THE SECOND DRAFT

Practical Strategies to Revamp Five Key Areas in Your Life

THE SECOND DRAFT

How to Lead and Inspire Your Own Evolution

MIA NAKAT, PHD

"I know you are tired - but come, this is the way."
-Rumi

CONTENTS

FOREWORD

Dr. Mia Nakat has been both a friend and mentor dating back to my "pre-doctor" life. I met Dr. Nakat just before beginning my journey through medical school. Not only is she down-to-earth and pragmatic, but she is also refreshingly warm and responsive in an industry driven by hard data and results. Dr. Nakat is the greatest personal and professional cheerleader you could imagine!

For example, Dr. Nakat was researching and educating people to be careful of toxins and endocrine disrupting compounds long before these were household words. She understands that our daily decisions, and the exposures to our environments, can impact our lives for years to come.

In true Dr. Nakat fashion, *The Second Draft* beautifully and succinctly merges information for both left-brained and right-brained folks.

It is with great honor that I now write the foreword to her debut book, a hands-on "How To" self-improvement guide with a dash of science thrown in.

The intersection of self-care and self-help is reimagining yourself - and therefore your life.

The impacts of managing your physical and emotional environment, taking control of your time, and building upon your strengths for your personal "brand" all affect how you FEEL and how you LIVE. These impacts are synonymous with robust mental health.

I once read that Steve Jobs wore the same outfit to work every day (black turtleneck, jeans, and sneakers) to minimize the number of decisions he had to make about his wardrobe. *The average adult makes 35,000 decisions per day.* Imagine how much can be simplified by having routine, programmed shortcuts in our daily life, thus saving cognitive space for our more important decisions. As Dr. Nakat points out in Chapter Four, keeping it simple really does work. Overthinking is a huge time sink, energy sink, confidence drain, and impediment to progress.

There is no question that the COVID-19 pandemic created an adverse experience in most of our lives, whether by fear related to the illness itself, or the isolation and life-disrupting changes to our social architecture.

As a psychiatrist, I see daily in my practice the lifelong impact of Adverse Childhood Experiences (ACEs) on physical and mental health. Adversity breaks down into three categories: abuse, neglect, and household dysfunction. Experiences such as getting bullied, going through the divorce of your parents, growing up around substance abuse or addiction, losing a parent by death or abandonment, physical or sexual abuse, or witnessing domestic violence all have immediate AND long-term impacts on one's physical and mental wellbeing. We call this "Toxic Stress." Research shows that people with ACEs have higher rates of diseases such as obesity, diabetes, heart disease, cancer, depression, suicide attempts, and addiction as compared to the general population.

As a contributor to our local NPR station, I frequently discuss the intersection of physical and mental health. We are just beginning to scratch the surface of how physical health affects mental health and vice versa. For example, people who have seizures tend to get MORE seizures if they are stressed out, sleep deprived, or physically sick. Then, having more seizures leads to worse daily functioning and increased rates of depression and anxiety. The same applies to migraines, autoimmune conditions, and disruptions to our gut's naturally occurring bacteria. So, yes, you can "worry yourself sick."

The good news is, Positive Childhood Experiences (PCEs) outweigh the impact of Toxic Stress. The seven PCEs are: 1) Able to talk with my family about my feelings. 2) Felt that my family stood by me during difficult times. 3) Enjoyed participating in community traditions. 4) Felt a sense of belonging in high school. 5) Felt supported by friends. 6) Had at least two non-parent adults who took a genuine interest in me. 7) Felt safe and protected by an adult in my home.

Hmm... don't these PCEs sound a whole lot like the ideas Dr. Nakat, and Chapter Two contributing guest author Walid Ramady, bring forth to us ADULTS in *The Second Draft?* Dr. Nakat gives us life hacks to:

- -Improve our Human Quotients.
- -Establish motivation, willpower, and self-control in time management.
- -Grow through mentorship (giving and receiving mentorship).
- -Develop a supportive community.
- -Push past our discomfort to reach for what we need, and for what will make us better.
- -Acquire more confidence.

Just keep practicing until these changes become second nature!

As famous psychiatrist and psychoanalyst, Dr. Carl Jung said, *"I am not what happened to me, I am what I choose to become."* This is what Dr. Nakat's book is all about!

So curl up and get ready for the book equivalent of a fireside chat with your brilliant best friend/role model/mentor and enjoy *The Second Draft!*

Sandra Vexler, MD
ABPN Board Certified
Adult and Child & Adolescent Psychiatrist

INTRODUCTION
What Could Be

"Livie, you are running the wrong way, stay in your lane, we talked about this." Livie's father was trying to keep her from colliding with other kids. She was running in circles on the track while waiting to pick up her older siblings from school.

Livie is five - almost five. She will soon learn that it is not okay to color outside the lines. She will know that running around haphazardly is not the safest or most productive.

By now, we have run the straight lines, strived to accomplish our projected goals, and settled into our roles and responsibilities on the track of life. What

1

comes next? The focus of this book's methodology is based on lifestyle improvements and creating meaningful life balance. *The Second Draft* does not represent medical opinions. Be sure to consult with your doctor before taking on any new changes.

> "A global study by Qualtrics found 42% of people have experienced a decline in mental health. Specifically, 67% of people are experiencing increases in stress while 57% have increased anxiety, and 54% are emotionally exhausted. 53% of people are sad, 50% are irritable, 28% are having trouble concentrating, 20% are taking longer to finish tasks, 15% are having trouble thinking and 12% are challenged to juggle their responsibilities." *Forbes, 2021*[1]

Depression and somber feelings are at an all-time high both at work and at home. Qualtrics described mental health as "the other COVID-19 crisis."[2] At a professional level, many employees are experiencing burnout. Burnout can be associated or confused with depression. The American Psychological Association (APA) describes burnout as a "physical, emotional, or mental exhaustion accompanied by decreased motivation, lowered performance, and negative attitudes toward oneself and others."[3]

Contradictory, our work driven culture proudly associates burnout signals with hard work and excellence.[4] Yet burnout is counterproductive to success. True excellence comes from efficient productivity and positive interactions with others.

Happiness requires harmony. We cannot attain harmony without work-life balance. We forget that companies play a large role in achieving this healthy balance for their employees for a win-win outcome.[5] Healthy, balanced employees can better execute in both their work and personal life. As a consequence, the employer benefits from creative, innovative, and resourceful employees who become excellent negotiators, critical thinkers, and problem solvers.[5] A tired workforce that is burned out is overworked, stressed, and unhappy - whether they are at home or in the office. They lose their sense of harmony and purpose. The world around them either becomes monotone and routine with work stress or becomes chaotic and unpredictable in an overwhelming way.

The COVID-19 pandemic has cooped us up in our routines and new normals. *We re-emerge into an inflated culture and economy.* There is a great resignation all around us, and our coping skills are suffering. How can I even measure my success? Am I happy? I feel disconnected yet overwhelmed. Am I in a rut? How am I even relevant? I cannot even relate! I feel depleted.

By the time we graduate from high school, we would have spent thousands of hours receiving instructions and building up our skills and character with the support of educators. After college, we continue to grow and mature in the work field. Some of us are blessed to have mentors along the way. However, many adults lack mentors in various stages of their lives. Mentors can provide a framework for open and trusted communications, accountability, and competency.

Mentorship can come from peers, professional networks, counselors, relatives, or religious leaders. Yet the idea of adults receiving one-on-one mentorship seems to be overshadowed by busy schedules and the presence of influencers stealing the spotlight. Even when companies assign supervisors, team members on projects, or someone to shadow, they do not formalize the importance of being mentored.

When is the last time you approached someone you respect to ask them to be your mentor? With many of us working from home or in hybrid schedules, it is even more challenging to establish that mentor-mentee relationship. Mainly because we are not observing this person interacting with daily situations. This is especially true for young adults out of college who have transitioned from having advisors, counselors, coaches, professors, and research directors to simply having a boss at a new job.

Would you like to be a mentor? Being a mentor is also rewarding not just for the mentee, but also for the development of the leadership skills of the mentor. Mentors are more open minded, understand various viewpoints, help with problem solving, and are great at organizational development. Mentors also have powerful skill sets in their profession that they can pass on to next generations. Right now, as an example, there is a skilled talent shortage in healthcare, education, and many industries; especially in infrastructure, manufacturing, and utilities.[6,7,8,9]

There is a loss of critical industry knowledge and experienced professionals entering the market. These industries not only appreciate skilled labor and degreed graduates, but they also offer high paying salaries. Yet there is a disconnect between existing leadership and the number of incoming workers growing into the different fields. Even with new digital infrastructure transformations, hands-on technical and leadership skills remain critical to the success of our nation and economy.[10,11] So what is missing?

Leaders like you!

Do not doubt your skills and accomplishments. This is the time to repackage yourself to fit in better and re-emerge into your confident and successful leadership role. You have so much to give, and will always have more to learn. It is a win-win situation. Are you ready for your second draft? Let's go...

PRACTICAL STRATEGIES
TO REVAMP FIVE KEY AREAS IN YOUR LIFE

We should always be in draft mode. Ready to learn and better ourselves. The work you invested early in your studies and career - your first draft - made you the amazing person you are today. *The Second Draft* will help re-inspire you and reconnect you. This book will spark that fire of motivation you know you still have somewhere for both your personal and professional life. This is not a book that addresses you as only the professional, or only personal. *The Second Draft* addresses you as a person who is trying to do it all. Doing your best to do it all. You are weary and deserve to refocus and rebalance by investing in yourself, so you can be there for everything and everyone else.

The Second Draft is an easy-to-apply, practical, step-by-step guide to help you repackage yourself for today's world in a meaningful way. The holistic approach covers various aspects that can affect your physical and mental wellbeing.

The five key areas are communication, productivity, the built environment, marketing yourself, and socialization.

This book is a quick read, all-encompassing (five books in one), and not overwhelming. You will find inner peace and balance again.

You can start with one topic or multiple topics at once. You can pick and choose or modify what works best for you. The objective is to be confident and inspired by the changes and growth you are witnessing within yourself.

In this fast paced society, we are rapidly reeled into and twittered through ideas and information. When considering a typical word count in this book genre, many books require a quiet vacation so the reader can have enough time to read the entire manuscript. If you are short on time, no worries. This book is practical and flexible in both structure and magnitude of topics. Some publishing agents recommend a one topic "big book" typed with extensive research accumulations, while other agents applaud an easy to read workable guidebook. I provided you the best of both.

The ✅ **TRY THIS** section at the end of each chapter is backed by hours of scientific research yet summarized into action items so you can start applying the recommendations immediately. So dive right ahead with the actionable items and go back and forth to the literature and academic resources found in the body of each chapter. Whatever you prefer. Or read the book in sequence and see how it all ties up together. Even better, at the end of the book, you can access a compilation of the recommendations under the **SUMMARY CHECKLIST**. These recommendations are not complicated. They are straightforward ideas you can try out, practice, and be mindful of throughout your day.

In the age of influencers, being influenced by your own measures is key to confident living and self-satisfaction. Reinventing yourself after the unstable times we witnessed in the pandemic can be confusing. Fitting in and interacting seems difficult. Some of us have even lost loved ones and we deal with complicated grief, while others are living with new disabilities. Many of us lost friends that could not relate to our grief or experiences that we faced in the last couple of years. Some even made new friends that were better aligned with their thinking on social, political, economic, and even religious topics. In general, though, it seems like we were barely thriving. Know that you are not alone in this feeling.

We can get frustrated by being complacent with ourselves and unmotivated for what lies ahead. These emotions are normal and natural. Look at you, you are already doing something about it. Give yourself due credit.

As you read this book, have a pen nearby. Use the **SUMMARY CHECKLIST** at the end of the book to help you keep track of and jot down ideas that you are inspired to try out.

Each chapter will guide you on how to direct yourself to be the successful, confident, and happy leader you know the world needs more of. You will find yourself again. You will harmonize with your surroundings in your own comfortable way.

This book is about being inspired by your own evolution and quietly showing the world how it is done.

CHAPTER ONE
The Fortune Teller

Did you know that Twitter doubled the character limit from 140 to 280 in November of 2017? Two hundred and eighty characters, that is what you get…go ahead express yourself. Make a point. Be impactful. Stand out. Caption a meme and video stream a reel. Instant communication, instant gratification. We can all agree that communicating today is very different from what it used to be. We are okay with this style of communication. It is efficient, it is effective, and it saves us time.

But are we really understood when we "talk" to each

other?

In grade school, they taught us grammar, language arts, literature, and presentation in speech. Sure, critical thinking exercises helped us with reading comprehension. However, when did we learn "speaking" comprehension? What does the other person really mean by that?

This chapter is about better communication. It is about reading others and yourself.

If I were a fortune teller, I would be better at figuring out people's intentions. I would be able to read their minds and predict their actions. I could even look into my own future and lead my exchanges with the world to guarantee happiness and success. Too bad I am not a fortune teller! However, I can be mindful of how words and body cues can help me dictate better interactions. I can even influence these interactions I have with others.

Many amazing books on personality traits, love languages, and communication come with extensive research and application - mainly highlighting how we are different. We are different, yet we are similar in that we all want to be understood. We need to get to a consensus with others. This consensus will allow for more harmony in our lives, less stress, more productivity, and better relationships. We work on our IQ (Intelligence Quotient) skills throughout our lives and careers. When do we get to work on our EQ (Emotional Quotient), empathy, and understanding of others so we can be better understood? Researchers have identified many other quotients, below are just a few:

VARIOUS ELEMENTS OF THE HUMAN QUOTIENTS

EQ	Emotional Quotient
AQ	Adversity Quotient
SQ	Social Quotient
SQ	Spiritual Quotient
SQ	Skills Quotient
CQ	Creative Quotient
DQ	Digital Quotient
VQ	Vision Quotient
IQ	Intelligence Quotient

EQ helps us with empathy and the ability to identify and manage our own emotions, in addition to the emotions of others. EQ is critical for us to be able to relate well with others and society as a whole. If we cannot relate to others, we are not able to communicate effectively and demonstrate our true intentions. For many that identify as empaths, they argue that these emotions might be too strong and overwhelming. The objective of this chapter is to balance these emotions and our thoughts no matter what array you fall under. More importantly, this chapter will make you aware of your AQ (Adversity Quotient) and encourage you to be resilient and patient with yourself and other people and situations. By doing so, you can adapt your communication style to be better understood by recognizing and understanding your surrounding cues. But first, let us better understand EQ and AQ.

Definition of Emotion

"A conscious mental reaction (such as anger or fear) subjectively experienced as strong feeling usually directed toward a specific object and typically accompanied by physiological and behavioral changes in the body"[1]

Definition of Adversity

"A state or instance of serious or continued difficulty or misfortune"[1]

These definitions are unfortunately easy for us to understand because we have all experienced occurrences that have led to, and triggered, many painful feelings within us. Here in Texas, we faced two 100-year events all at once in 2021. We called it SNOWVID, a historic winter snow storm and a virus outbreak all at once. We lost critical power and access to many roads and resources. People died. Markets started selling T-shirts that had, "I survived SNOWVID" written on them. *A few hailstorms followed, that shattered our windshields, and whatever was left of our patience and resilience.* Still today, in the aftermath of a pandemic, current news are filled with violence and extreme weather events. Stress is all around us. How we deal with our emotional state can show our resilience and strength.

How we understand others' differences in dealing with their adversity and emotions will also highlight our kindness and leadership. For example, in a recent study,[2] empathy was considered the most important leadership skill. The study highlights that empathetic leaders are able to boost positive outcomes, such as innovation and engagement, and reduce burnout. With a more empathetic leader, employees feel respected, included, valued, and have a better hold on work-life balance. This results in better retention rates and a more productive work environment that is less burdensome on mental health and wellness.[2]

Even pets within our household, such as our dogs, our most loyal creatures, are documented to show empathy. When a dog's parent gets injured or stumbles around; many dogs will also start limping! Have you ever witnessed this mimicking behavior in pets? Why is that?

This mimicking behavior is known as "emotional contagion,"[3] dogs and other social species will pick up on your mood, behavior, and body language. The injury mirroring is known as "automatic imitation."[4]

Humans exhibit this unconscious mirroring behavior as well. Social species are very observant and can pick up habits they are regularly exposed to consciously and subconsciously. Something as simple as yawning can initiate spontaneous mimicry. Recent research compared facial mimicry and contagious yawning to emotional contagion. The author concluded that the yawning was not specifically driven by emotional contagion. The yawning was mainly driven by "biased attentional processes and yawn detection rather than emotional sharing."[5] So what does that tell us? It tells us that being present in our actions and attention influences our behavior and how others perceive us. Consequently, our behaviors and perception influence how people treat us.

Fast forward to social media content and the power of persuasion. In the Journal of Business Research, the authors researched the power of persuasion and emotional contagion in the success of social media influencers. Linguistic style and emotional contagion were central to the popularity and success of the influencer.[6] This again shows that *people are persuaded by our words and actions, even if witnessed through a screen.*

For some of us, being emotional and empathetic is too much of a good thing - it drains us. For a Highly Sensitive Person (HSP)[7] or a person with Sensory Processing Sensitivity (SPS),[8] it is important to set boundaries and regulate our own emotions. HSP and SPS are not diseases or disorders, they are temperament traits. On the contrary, self-awareness and recharge are important for people with these qualities because they care and give so much of their emotions to others. It does not make them weaker; it makes them emotionally stronger. Environmental awareness and supportive surroundings are important ways to recharge. Chapter Three is dedicated to this topic and very helpful for everyone, especially people with high SPS.

ADVERSE EVENTS

When it comes to adversity, understanding why some individuals are more resilient than others is very complex and depends on many psychological and neurobiological variables. However, *one theme remains critical for creating a more resilient individual: social support.*[9] This is why Chapter Five is solely dedicated to developing this aspect of your life.

Think about it. Most people you know, yourself included, must have endured at least one or two trauma exposures in a span of a lifetime. We can learn from each other's experiences. Traumas change us, for good or bad, they do. We try to grow through our traumatic experiences and we learn how to support others in overcoming theirs. For some of us, trauma can be very detrimental. It takes time to heal. Healing takes time and effort, support and resources, and the big will to overcome. Grief is an example of such trauma. We all have our own timeline and behavior on how to go through losing someone we love, and it gets complicated! Yes, literally a term called "complicated grief,"[10] when we are stuck in our sadness.

Grief and bereavement are the ultimate shared experience. Grief is expressed as an emotional reaction to a loss, while bereavement is the period of grief and mourning after the loss. Many cultures even have set rituals to engage in grief on a social scale. Yet, for many, grief is a very isolating and lonely place. Not only because of the loss but also due to the confrontation of morality; and the coping with the new anxieties that come from this experience of missing someone so much. Eventually, we all need to heal. When healing is impeded, and grief is intense and prolonged, complicated grief needs to be addressed.[10] Our loved ones will always be missed. The sadness of not having them in our lives will always be there. However, complicated grief that is ongoing and detrimental requires attention and care.

Other than pharmacotherapy (medicine), a specific technique in cognitive behavioral therapy is promising when dealing with complicated grief.

More specifically, a University of California San Diego technique includes a type of prolonged exposure of "repeatedly telling the story of the death and in vivo exposure activities" and asking the patient to focus on personal goals and relationships.[11]

These sessions are not easy, and they include homework outside the one-on-one meetings. The sixteen-session protocol is impressive and organized in its method. To include inviting a "supportive person" to one of the sessions and focusing on the "potential for reawakening the capacity for joy..."[11] In the third session, the supportive friend or partner visiting is asked to "describe the client since the death, his or her reactions to grief, and any avoided situations or activities."[11] This is an especially arduous task. When the aggrieved hears their loved ones' impacts due to their partner's sadness, it is very moving. For me, it is revealing, and it pushes me to be stronger to protect my loved ones and my surroundings from my grief and sadness.

Deaths that are sudden and unexpected are particularly difficult. Some losses are met with "silent grief," where the grieving feel obliged to hide their emotions and carry on while others are not receptive to their pain. Sibling loss[12] and miscarriages can be examples of "silent grief." They are very lonely places to be. Social support and understanding could be of great help. It is important to note that grief is not depression:

> "Depression inhibits the capacity to experience positive emotions. Grief does not...Depression biases thinking in a negative direction. Grief does not. Depression interferes with the capacity to care about other people and to understand their good intentions. Grief turns a person inward, but the desire to be with others and appreciation for the efforts of others is preserved." *M. K. Shear, 2022*[10]

So give yourself grace and recognize symptoms of grief or burnout in your life. Both could exhibit sadness that is confused and associated with depression. Depression, on the other hand, can co-occur with various other experiences. Self-awareness and resources are important aspects of addressing all the above. There is no cookie-cutter approach or timeline that should constrict you. Set goals and be intentional about getting better and do something about it. Have a plan. Some days will be better than others, so do not focus on any hiccups. Focus on the long-term projection and quality improvements along the way.

BOUNCING BACK

Resilience is difficult without self-compassion and social support. To conquer both, one must have self-understanding and good relationships with others. These relationships cannot happen without proper communication, which is the theme of this chapter.

Trying to understand the pillars of resilience is not easy from a scientific perspective. This is due to variations in our neuropsychological traits and upbringing. Yet many themes have emerged consistently, such as:

- Resiliency is centered on our ability to preserve or bounce back our psychological health and normal functioning after going through adverse events.[13]

- Self-compassion, social support, and positive emotions are important.[13]

- Intervention programs can increase our success in facing adversities and improve our AQ.[14]

- Your AQ can be measured by the Adversity Response Profile (ARP). You can improve your resilience and have more success and happiness in life.[15]

- When faced with hardships, many give up before "they have tested their limits and contributed their utmost."[15]

The term AQ and the ARP assessment was coined by Paul Stoltz, PhD in 1997.[15] Dr. Stoltz highlights how AQ is an indicator of success and behaviors towards stress and adversities. He has written multiple books on this important topic and is considered the world's leading authority on the integration and application of grit and resilience.[16] He now leads a learning company called PEAK Learning where you can find many resources on the topic.[16] Something notable about Dr. Stoltz is that he was inspired by his resilient grandmother who lived for 106 years.[17] Some of his most remarkable findings when it comes to AQ are that your AQ can be improved, regardless of age. The key to AQ is measuring and strengthening how you respond to situations.

The tool Dr. Stoltz uses to improve AQ is focused on answering these CORE questions. C = Control, to what extent can you influence whatever happens next to a situation you are facing, whether it is your fault or not? O = Ownership, how likely will you step up and do something about the problem to make it better? R = Reach, to what magnitude do you perceive this will reach into and affect everything else? E = Endurance, how long do you perceive the duration of this situation to last?[18]

Most importantly, Dr. Stoltz encourages you to not feel helpless and doubt your control over an obstacle that you are faced with. Instead, convert the adversity to a propelling power and show up to face adversity. It builds your character and leaves a legacy behind.[18] Just be patient and have faith that the adversity might just be good for you in the long run. If you lose a job, you can land a better one. A partner breaks up with you, you find yourself in love with someone who values you even more.

Adversities might just be what push you to an even better life for yourself. Do not sit down and do nothing about a problem you are facing. You are free to rightfully mope around a few days, minutes, months...whatever it takes for you to determine that this adversity will not define you in a negative way. Instead, it will define your actions for future successes and lessons learned. We repeatedly hear stories of perseverance from now successful authors, athletes, business entrepreneurs, immigrants, and billionaires who have faced one tragedy and rejection after another. Yet, they persevere. So can you.

Do you see the themes forming? Understanding, emotions, adversities, resilience, grief, social support, self-compassion, empathy, leadership, emotional contagion, persuasion, and patience! All these traits require communication and interaction with others. They are hard to learn in school. The school of life makes us aware of these emotions, in good and bad. Many of us are not accustomed to talking about feelings, let alone sharing our inner thoughts with others; especially in a professional or social setting. I am not asking you to become uncomfortably emotional or dramatic with your dealings, or an open book to all or any. On the contrary, I am asking you to be a strong leader, starting with leading your own path to success and happiness regardless of the situation in front of you. There is a balanced way, a measured response, on how we communicate with one another while keeping our emotions in check. Depending solely on IQ is not sufficient.

We do not need a fortune teller to connect better with others, surround ourselves with a supportive environment, and practice better EQ and AQ. We can do this on our own. Let us try this...

⊘ TRY THIS: CONNECT BETTER WITH YOUR PEOPLE, CONNECT BETTER WITH YOURSELF!

Acknowledge Your Own Resilience: Being resilient takes time. It is hard work. As we go through adversity, it is difficult to see the potential lessons learned and adaptability evolution that we harbor through the process. This is why acknowledging our resilience is so important. *Acknowledging our resilience allows us to recognize the power we create as we go through negative experiences.* Our self-awareness assures us that it is okay to feel distressed. With time and intentionality, we can overcome our negative thoughts, connect better with compassionate people that can validate our feelings, and be proactive about our life's purpose.[19]

By becoming more empathetic towards yourself first, you will become more empathetic towards the needs and experiences of others. Acknowledge your circumstances. Accept your sadness, fear, and any other emotional response. Accepting your emotional reaction will help you manage it better - with grace towards yourself. Reducing the load of these emotions within you will grant you the patience to understand the troubles others are going through (some gracefully and some not so much).

Close your eyes. Breathe. Visualize yourself as a child. Explain to this child the tribulations the years will bring. The ups, the downs, the wins, and the losses. Do not be sad. Focus on the kindness, care, and gentleness of your inner voice as you talk to this child. Using that same concern and tone your inner voice gave this child, now redirect it to yourself. Give yourself the promise that "even though you have gone through so much, you are strong and you will be resilient." Open your eyes.

Acknowledge this kindness you just granted yourself. Remember that others may need this same gesture, whether they know it or not. Who knows what their troubles are, and how far they have come. Focus on the progress and actions you continue to take to propel yourself forward in life, despite all the setbacks. Stay determined and know that it is normal to have setbacks. Rinse and repeat.

Verbally Ask For and Offer Help: Ask for help to understand others when there is a gap in communication or conflict. Simply ask, "please explain this so I can better understand it?" When you see people burdened at work or in life by the simplest or most critical tasks, lend a hand by asking, "how can I make this better for you?"

When life sends you adversity, do not shut down emotionally. Take a break, reflect in silence, and then ask for what could make you feel better. Ask for grace when you need it, "I am having a hard time dealing with my circumstance, I appreciate your patience and support." You may not be able to "fix" someone's problem. Others may not be able to "fix" your problem either. At least, there will be better understanding and patience among all. It will amaze you how simple gestures can make all the difference in how people view your support. More so, reaching out and asking for help can guide others who want to help you but do not know how. No circumstance is too trivial or too severe for you to not reach out. Again, validate your own emotions and acknowledge your resilience. The same applies to how you view others. Do not minimize other people's adversities and the emotions they associate with, even if their circumstances seem minor compared to yours.

Mimicking and Mirroring: Mimicking and mirroring have been praised and researched as a major form of nonverbal communication that leads to rapport. We discussed emotional contagion. Take note, I am not asking you to purposely imitate the body language, speech, or facial expressions of others. Mirroring is usually a subconscious effort. However, even in infancy, we were born to mimic others around us. By imitation, we learn to talk and behave. So how do you go about fitting into your surroundings without - let us face it - seeming weird copying others? The answer is to be well prepared for your interactions, events, and surroundings ahead of time.

There is a form of formality that we have lost in recent years because we are protected by the keyboard or screen. Working from home, we are more casual and "comfortable in our own skin." Being confident and comfortable is actually very important. However, this comfort cannot be misused in situations where we need to be aware of our social context. For example, be aware of dress code, diversity of races and cultural backgrounds, and how comfortable others are with various verbal and nonverbal communication styles.

Be aware of and understand people's personality traits. Are they loud? Are they quiet? Are they serious? Or, do they love joking around? Also, be conscious of generational differences in communication. *Different age groups have experienced life events in various ways. We have different triggers, drivers, and expressions.* If at any point you feel confused about why the interaction feels heavy, take a step back. Recognize that you might be communicating based on your generational viewpoints. Be respectful and try to understand. Sometimes you can reach a consensus. Sometimes you can compromise. Sometimes you can respectfully agree to disagree. The key word is showing respect and the willingness to hear someone out. Whatever their way or form of communication or the intent of it is, as long as it is respectful.

I am not asking you to change who you are to accommodate others. *I am not asking you to be reserved and/or afraid to express yourself. I am asking you to be prepared for the environment and interaction you will be undertaking so you are well received and well understood.*

One of my favorite examples of nonverbal communication is the pandemic nametags used in conferences/in-person meetings. These stickers signal if you are comfortable shaking hands, fist bumping, or just saying hello without any touching.

I remember early on in the pandemic trying to figure out the foot tap/elbow shake dance we were introduced to as the new greeting norm. I remember losing my balance and accidentally kicking one of my Texas-booted colleagues so hard that my foot hurt for a week afterward. Soon enough, I tried finding alternative greeting methods where my line dancing abilities were not required.

I wish life came with sticker guides. Sadly, we do not have life-guide stickers. If we did, I would be walking around sticking them (actually many of them) on my forehead. For now, being aware of your surroundings and keeping that formality until you naturally integrate with others around you subconsciously is our next best alternative. I am not asking you not to stand out and be yourself. I am telling you to show your leadership skills with grace by truly connecting, understanding, listening, and showing empathy to others. This way, you show respect. *With respect comes rapport, better communication, better engagement, and more successful relationships.*

Regulate Your Response During Conflict: Sometimes we find ourselves in less desirable situations. If at any time you feel unsafe in a space, leave and call authorities immediately. This section is about regulating your responses during encounters that can arise in negotiations, personal relationships, customer service, and other situations that do not indicate any danger. There is zero tolerance for any danger or violence. Debates and dialogues are part of our normal interactions in society. Voicing viewpoints is how we intermingle with others. Our thoughts can set us up to be influential and successful leaders that are well respected and praised.

Exercise patience. "Take note of this: everyone should be quick to listen, slow to speak and slow to become angry."[20] I know, it is difficult to do so. Count silently and slowly to 11 (because 10 is not always enough)! Yes, pause and silently count to 11:

1, 2, 3, 4, 5, 6, 7, 8, 9, 10, 11.

Now breathe and verbalize clearly. Do not talk too fast or slow, do not mumble, and do not raise your voice. Nothing is more frustrating than having a discussion with someone and not being able to follow their thoughts because you are distracted by their voice tone. So check yourself, articulate, and genuinely control your tone. Chapter Four covers more details about vocals and voice tone. If the other person is not speaking clearly, at a pause simply let them know, "I was not able to follow your thoughts, would you please repeat that and help me better understand?" Usually, just asking this question allows the person you are having the discussion with to evaluate their speech pattern. Validate the interaction by repeating what you understood and allow the other person time to respond to correct you if you misinterpreted their intent. Also notice, that you used an "I" statement. You indicated "I was not able to understand ..." you spoke for yourself.

Use "I" statements to describe your thoughts and feelings. Do not use accusatory "you" statements, such as "you are misinformed." Instead rephrase and say "I received different information x, y, and z." Be patient and be specific in the way you articulate your feelings and points across to be better understood. Let your kindness and knowledge shine through, instead of your loud voice and anger. *"Raise your words, not your voice. It is rain that grows flowers, not thunder."* Rumi.

Never Look Back at Toxic People: Give yourself the permission and the relief of parting ways with toxic people. Say it with me, "toxic people, you are dismissed from my life." Wait a minute! What if these people are family members, neighbors, or colleagues that you have to see all the time? It is simple (awkward but simple): minimize, avoid, reduce, and be formal in all interactions with them. You cannot control people's behaviors, but you can choose to not be engaged in all of them. More so, some people you just do not have good chemistry with. This does not make you a bad person, or vice versa. Of course, request and work on a resolution or try to find middle ground first. When it comes to toxic situations, unfortunately, those resolutions do not always come through despite all your best efforts.

It may seem to you that I am encouraging you to

not face relationship issues. In relationships worth saving, issues may be resolved by counseling and with efforts from both parties. When relationships become toxic, they are usually a one way conflict where the other person is unaware and unwilling to change. Regrettably, these types of relationships are better off avoided or minimized. Keeping interactions at a minimum will reduce the negative feelings you experience in their presence. *This is not because you are an unkind person. It is because you are granting yourself and the other person the respect of a conflict-free relationship.* Some traits to look out for in toxic relationships include:

- People that dismiss how their words and actions impact you. They may find it funny and playful to repeatedly make you feel a certain way. Even when you make them aware of how their action is hurting your feelings or disrespecting you.

- One way relationships in which you are the one always giving, compromising, and providing the support.

- Toxic relationships can be subtle and not

physically abusive. Relationships that are silently abusive, such as passive aggressiveness, silent treatment, word jabs, belittling statements, and manipulative techniques are all toxic traits.

• In general, you are not at ease around this person. For no specific reason, you might dread meeting and seeing this person. You may feel obliged in the relationship. You come up with excuses to not interact. Again, it does not make you or them a bad person; you are just better off disconnecting from this relationship. Sometimes the chemistry is just not there and you are both better off not being part of the other person's life.

The objective of this chapter was to offer verbal and non-verbal communication concepts that you can implement starting today to be better understood. Being empathetic and resilient is hard work. This is why balancing your surroundings and getting relief from toxic situations is important for your physical and mental wellbeing.

The concepts covered will help you read others

and yourself in a conflict-free and meaningful way. They will help you be more confident in your interactions as I discuss further in Chapter Four. Sometimes we are in an internal conflict with our own thoughts. We may be confused about what is best for us, which can bring us a fear of the unknown and anxiety. Work through this book to invest time in your own needs. Start by better knowing yourself. You can have better and more fulfilling interactions with others when you are more comfortable in your own skin. Even in the early 1900s, the Nobel Prize winner, scientist Marie Curie, highlighted the importance of being understood. *"Nothing in life is to be feared, it is only to be understood. Now is the time to understand more, so that we may fear less."*

CHAPTER TWO
The More Time I Have

The more time I have, the more disorganized I seem!
This chapter is about productivity, not only at work,
but for your personal life as well. Spending the time
where you need it, to make time for where you want
it!

First things first. Go ahead and turn your cellphone
ringer on. Gasp! What?! Yes, go ahead and turn your
cellphone ringer on. You read correctly. I know, I
know. We have had our ringers off since we stopped
using those cool Nokia tunes. So why am I telling you
to turn your ringers back on?

We keep reaching to our cellphones to check if we

missed silenced notifications - it is very distracting. Do not be alarmed, this is temporary. You will turn your ringer back off. First, you have to set up your VIP (Very Important Person) contacts and turn on important notifications. This way if your kid's school, your boss, your doctor, your significant other, elderly parent, best friend etc. needs to contact you, their number will bypass your silenced ringer. Now that you have selected critical notifications to bypass, you can turn your cellphone ringer back off. The same way you can select important notifications, you can also select to DND (Do Not Disturb) and mute unimportant ones.

You can now stop reaching for your cellphone resting assured that you will not miss important calls or messages. Sure, you cannot predict or set up every doctor, pharmacist, banker or insurance agent to your notification VIP contact list. So on days you are waiting on specific callbacks, it is okay to turn your cellphone ringer back on. Do not be loud or rude in meetings. Make sure the ringer is low enough for you to hear it without being disruptive to others. Excuse yourself quietly or if necessary say, "Excuse me while I take this important call I have been waiting on." Have your voicemail set up so it can receive messages if you do miss this critical call you have been waiting on.

While you are at it, go ahead and start unsubscribing from spam email. It might take you a few weeks but it is well worth it at the end to find a much more useful inbox. Most emails now have a one click, rapid unsubscribe, at the top or bottom of each email.

Technology and social media have provided us with instant communication and instant gratification. The same technology has also created a very distracting environment. We need to use our digital devices to aid our productivity as opposed to interrupting and extending our days. For that we turn to my contributing guest author, Walid Ramady, who has used intricate tools and software applications his entire career to help us break down simple, everyday habits of productivity. There is always room for improved time management when it seems that there are not enough hours in a day.

The Cambridge Dictionary defines productivity as: "The rate at which a person, company or country does useful work."[1] A significant word in this definition is "rate," which involves time as a factor. It is tied to the amount of work one produces during a measurable period of time.

Interruptions play a role in impacting efficiency; they are ubiquitous and inescapable. Interruptions can be separated into two categories, external and internal. External interruptions stem from your surrounding environments such as acquaintances, noise, phone calls, or unexpected meetings. A colleague, for example, drops by to have a chat. This results in disrupting your focus regardless of how you handle the interruption.

Internal interruptions, on the other hand, are tied to habits and self-control. They consist of our internal tendencies to switch focus from the current task to unrelated matters. For example, checking updates on social media (or other forms of electronic communication) has now become integrated into our internal daily habits.

We experience both forms of interruptions (external and internal) when working on a task. It is the amount and impact of these interruptions that may be surprising. According to a 2019 study,[2] we experience interruptions, or task switching, on average every three minutes. These interruptions not only impact your performance, but also result in an increased likelihood of errors, stress development, higher workload, added frustration, and increased time pressure. Once the distraction is over, it takes a whopping 23 minutes on average to resume the activity at hand.[3]

FACTORS THAT IMPACT PRODUCTIVITY

Poor Sleep: According to the Journal of Occupational and Environmental Medicine,[4] poor sleep disrupts the productivity of employees. A lack of proper sleep not only impacts your performance for the next day, but it also continues doing so in the upcoming days as well.

Disengagement from Work: More than 70% of the workforce exhibits passive or active disengagement.[5] This infers that most of the workforce experiences a lack of interest in their current role or company. Disengagement harms productivity, but more importantly it also negatively impacts the organization they work for. Stay engaged at work; keep in mind that work engagement contributes to productivity, sense of accomplishment, and ultimately your success.

The term "engaged"[6] employees refers to workers that are enthusiastic and dedicated to the organization they work for. Engaged employees often display a high level of participation and eagerness toward the success of their company. These professionals go beyond expectations to help their company succeed. A 2021 study[7] found that good relationships and communication between employees and management improve the level of engagement. Meaningful work has also been found to contribute to employees' engagement.[8] Seek meaningful work in your career. If the work you are performing today does not seem to be meaningful, raise your voice and ask to be given different responsibilities that are aligned with your values.

Multitasking: A 2020 article published by Forbes[9] notes that *multitasking can reduce productivity* by as much as 40%. This number may come as a surprise, as it breaks the general notion that multitasking is a skill that increases productivity. Keep this in mind the next time you find yourself working on various activities simultaneously.

Stress: According to a PWC report,[10] stress impacts employees as it reduces their productivity. Whether stress stems from work pressure or other sources, it results in an impact on your performance. Simply put, increased levels of stress result in lower productivity.[11] Finding ways to reduce stress in our daily lives is imperative. Another study[12] concludes that actively engaging in stress reduction techniques (such as progressive muscle relaxation) can reduce this stress and anxiety in our daily life.

Meditation and other guided stress reduction methods are practical and effective for improving your wellbeing. Stress reduction can be exercised regardless of where you are. Stress reduction is not only beneficial for your health and wellbeing but also your personal relationships. People who meditated improved their performance and relationship with management and their peers in the workplace.[13]

Work Pressure: According to The Yerkes-Dodson law,[14] performance increases with more work stress, but only up to a certain point. After which, productivity starts to drop as more pressure continues to build up. Poor performance can also be observed when little work pressure is experienced. Balancing the amount of work stress you need and can tolerate will help you maintain a strong performance.

There are various effective methods and tips you can use to help boost and optimize your productivity skills:

✅ TRY THIS: FOCUS. DONE. ENJOY!

Protect Your Time: It is seemingly harder to stay away from our smartphones, screens, or monitors. With the advent of the internet, information has become more accessible than ever before. The deluge of information stems from sources such as social media, 24-hour news cycles, stock markets, and more. We feel bombarded with information and are constantly tempted to switch focus away from the task at hand. Media multitasking, which can be defined as the act of checking different media platforms simultaneously, "has been associated with decreased cognitive control abilities and negative psychosocial impacts such as depression, social anxiety, negative social wellbeing, and even poor academic performance."[15]

Below are some ways that can help you reduce or manage these internal interruptions:

- Temporarily block digital media: DND options, discussed in the introduction of this chapter, serve as an efficient way to stop you from checking these distractions. Silencing your smartphone, airplane mode, or moving your electronic devices to a different room are another way. We are all unique and respond to these solutions differently. *Discover the method that works best for you by trying the various options until you find the optimal one.*

- Close unused tabs: we can easily get inundated with multiple open tabs in a browser. This leads to unavoidable distraction as you surf through a multitude of pages. Set a target number of open tabs. Once you exceed that number, reflect on which ones you need for the task at hand, then close the rest. If you are concerned about losing the tabs you are about to close, save them and revert to them later. You can also reprioritize the tabs by sliding less important ones to the end. Keep the number of tabs at a manageable level and avoid multitasking, which will help accentuate your focus.

- Temporary recluse: find a temporary escape by

moving to an isolated room where you can control the visual and auditory factors. A meeting room, or dedicated private space, should do the trick. If there is a glass wall, then the visual distractions may persist. To avoid this, place your back facing the glazed area where possible. It also helps to place a note outside the room asking not to be disturbed. This method will not be effective if the electronic distractions persist.

- Block your time: In his book *The Time Bandit Solution*,[16] Edward G. Brown describes an effective way to manage interruptions from individuals close to you. The method requires you to negotiate a "time lock" with the disruptors. This results in an agreed upon period throughout the day where no disruptions from these individuals are to occur. This method will buy you the time needed to focus on your work without being concerned about attention loss.

Plan Your Day: Time management is defined as a "form of decision making used by individuals to structure, protect, and adapt their time to changing conditions."[17] Not only is time management a skill that you can learn to control and master, but it is also a tool to help you adapt to the dynamic world around you.

A 2021 meta-analysis found that time management has a positive contribution to one's mindset and satisfaction.[18] In contrast, workplace stress can lead to anxiety, depression, irritability, and fatigue.[19] Time management, on the other hand, was found to reduce workplace stress. Time management boosts your confidence (see Chapter Four for more on confidence). *Confidence and productivity are linked by the resulting success, accomplishment, and self-improvement you experience from both.*

A key practice to improving your productivity is to plan your day ahead. It is important to turn this practice into a daily habit. Planning ahead will provide clarity and knowledge of what needs to be accomplished. Planning allows you to optimize the energy and time you have. Lack of planning can lead to ineffective use of your time, allowing for distractions and lesser important tasks to take over where your focus ought to be. Below are some guidelines on how to plan your day.

- Assess yourself: start by assessing where you currently are in terms of effective time management. On a normal working day, be vigilant of your actions and surroundings. Note the time you spend working versus spending time on irrelevant tasks (distractions, phone calls, smartphone use, and more). At the end of the workday, compare what you should have accomplished and what you were able to complete. If you did not complete key tasks despite your best intentions in doing so, then ask yourself what you could have done differently to reach the original goals? Did the lesser critical activity really deserve your focus while you set aside more important opportunities? Do not forget to also ask yourself this: how can I do better tomorrow?

- Define your goals: at the start of your day, clearly define the goals you intend to meet by the end of it. Identifying the right goals and obtaining clarity on what you wish to achieve is crucial. Once identified, break your goals into manageable tasks and list them. Plan on scheduling some contingency time in your daily schedule for impromptu meetings, unexpected conversations, and problem solving. Your daily goals should fit in to successfully help you meet project deadlines, quarterly audits, or whatever long-term benchmarks your work requires. This planning effort will become more natural and less of a daily task as you get used to it.

- Estimate the work duration: from experience, try to estimate the time it takes to complete each activity. This time estimate will be based on the best information you have (historical data or benchmarking by referring to coworkers or similar projects).

- Develop your plan: create a schedule for the day by assigning a start and finish time for each task. This will be your plan for the day. If the schedule extends beyond the end of your workday, pick which tasks can be deferred to the next day. You need to ensure that your daily plan is realistic, manageable, and achievable. Do not lose sight of long-term goals and project deadlines. Do not forget to leave time for breaks and contingencies like we indicated before.

Keep in mind when developing your plan: 1) Be wary of the number of tasks you choose to tackle daily. Adding more responsibilities than you can handle could result in a counterproductive environment. 2) The urgency of the tasks you choose is another factor that plays a role in creating your daily list. It comes as no surprise that urgent tasks need to be on the list of things to complete by the end of the day. Yet, we tend to rank responsibilities with lower urgency for various reasons. Unless there is an emergency, try not to get swayed by outside distractions and stick to your plan. The lesser priority items should be handled only when there is time to do so. 3) When developing the schedule, make sure to leave room for unexpected disruptions. Uncertainties are a part of life that need to be included in your plan. 4) A study from the European Journal of Work and Organizational Psychology[20] describes that good sleep, combined with short breaks, plays a role in employee engagement in the workplace. Given these benefits, taking short rests throughout the workday should not be considered a waste of time, but rather a beneficial habit.

Throughout the day, revert to your schedule and assess your current status. If you are behind, simply update your plan to reflect the actual situation and continue working. Be wary of the reasons that caused the delay. Were you interrupted? If so, how much time did that take out from your plan? The planning process will become intrinsic and automatic the more you practice it.

Changes to your daily plan are to be expected. You may be dragged to an impromptu meeting or asked to address an urgent matter that takes priority over all else. Update your schedule and, if needed, make the concerned parties aware of the impact of this change on your original plan. If you work directly with management, make sure you leave enough time in your schedule for unexpected work events.

Reward yourself. An article from Cornell Chronicle[21] states that immediate rewards improve motivation. This is because rewards form an association between your effort and accomplishing your goals. This reward system is effective in boosting your motivation. The choice of the reward is up to you, be it walking outdoors, checking your social media account, indulging in a tasty snack, calling a friend, or any other activity that you enjoy. This will motivate you to work effectively to complete the task at hand so you can reward yourself. Do not be frugal with the reward if you are experiencing an especially busy day. Despite the pressure, it is still important to indulge every now and then so you can have the motivation to keep on going without burning out.

Influence Your Willpower: Mahatma Gandhi once said, "Strength does not come from physical capacity. It comes from an indomitable will." The path to achieving any goal starts when you develop a genuine desire to do so. Be it a need for a healthier regimen, learning a new language, or succeeding in your career; your willpower is the key driver on your road to betterment. It is a conscious power you can learn to influence and apply to get results.

To develop your willpower, you first need to ask yourself what you want, why, and how to reach it. After answering these questions, you will establish the end goal in mind. Having an end goal will guide and power your will. According to research,[22] strong performance might result from setting specific and challenging goals. It is thus imperative, when defining your end goal, to establish a clearly defined one. Your willpower is not only required to get you started, but is also needed through every step in your journey towards success.

Motivation and discipline are two factors that play a role in productivity.[23] Discipline and self-control influence your willpower. A study conducted on 140 eighth-grade students[24] showed that adolescents who did not perform as expected (relative to their IQ levels), did so because they lacked self-discipline. In the book *Willpower: Rediscovering the Greatest Human Strength*,[25] Roy Baumeister, PhD and John Tierney note that intelligence and self-control are identified as the most important factors needed to achieve success and happiness. While access to education can be limited, it is not so for self-control, which is a behavior that one can learn to manage from within. The philosopher Elbert Hubbard defined self-discipline as "the ability to make yourself do what you should do, when you should do it, whether you feel like it or not." Self-control is a skill we should learn to develop and use to focus on what we need while resisting the temptations and distractions around us. Discipline also leads to happiness, as it creates consistency. Discipline provides a feeling of purpose, achievement, and accomplishment while working on the desired goal.

Motivation is another driver of willpower. Motivation can be defined as the desire to reach a goal. Motivation represents your desire to succeed, an inner strength that should stay with you on your road to success. Being motivated is a constant reminder of the reason why we should overcome hardships. Motivation fuels determination by feeding it with purpose. Research was conducted over the span of 10 years on children's musical identity.[26] The children who had the desire to master their instruments had better chances of success than those who did not. *Practice alone may not make perfect. You need motivation to achieve ambitious goals and master a task or concept.*

In summary, motivation stems from your established end goals. Willpower then consciously allows you to put in place the needed actions, and self-control helps you stay on plan. For example, you form a desire (motivation) to strengthen your back muscles and reduce your chronic back pain (clearly defined goal). You consciously act upon this goal (using willpower) by making the time and effort to go to physical therapy. To succeed, you strictly follow the prescribed daily homework stretches and exercises (via self-control).

Avoid Procrastination: Avoiding procrastination is essential to maintaining good time management skills. The Roman philosopher Seneca once said, "Putting things off is the biggest waste of life: it snatches away each day as it comes and denies us the present by promising the future. The greatest obstacle to living is expectancy." Procrastination, which is defined as the act of deferring the undertaking of a task or action as late as possible, is a widespread tendency. Besides hampering your productivity, procrastination also adds stress. A study found that students who procrastinated showed a higher level of stress than those who did not.[27]

Present-bias is the act of preferring a short-term gain at the expense of a larger one in the future. For example, choosing unhealthy food today with the promise of eating better tomorrow; but when tomorrow comes, the cycle repeats itself. The reason for this present-bias behavior stems from the desire to achieve short-term gains. *When you procrastinate, you presume that your future self will one day do the hard work.* This was confirmed by the Stanford marshmallow experiment, conducted by psychologist Walter Mischel, PhD.[28] The famous study involved children who had a choice to make. Children were asked to choose between an immediate reward and a greater one if they waited longer. Having revisited the test subjects years on, Dr. Mischel found that there was a correlation between the SAT scores and the length of the wait for these treats. The longer the kids waited for their marshmallows, the more likely they were to obtain a higher exam score in the future. Those who waited also ranked higher in their social and cognitive functions than those who did not. This is likely because those who waited have developed more self-control over their present-bias. The study subjects understood that hard work today would provide more gains in the future.

There are a number of methods that can help you gain control over your decision-making process and prevent procrastination. One method is to trick yourself by committing to a plan that will come into effect later. Thus, giving the future you no option but to perform the task. An example of this is to enroll in a meal plan where you are left with no option but to eat the healthy meal already delivered. Another option is to remove the short-term rewards out of sight.

Finally, self-awareness can be exercised when presented with the option to procrastinate or labor today. Take control of your decision-making process by reminding yourself of the benefits of acting today. Project the intended goal in your mind to help remind you of the rewards you will reap from the efforts you are putting in now. Remember that you may not be available tomorrow for the tasks you are deferring. Today is indeed the best time to tackle your planned goals. The hard work you are exerting now will not go to waste.

Organize and Conquer: We face tasks and deadlines daily. The challenge of completing them on time may seem daunting or insurmountable. This section provides suggestions for making the most of our time and energy. Earlier, we covered the need to plan your day by breaking your goals into manageable tasks. Categorizing and prioritizing your short and long-term objectives is key to helping you achieve success.

What do you think is more productive, starting your day by working on the quickest activities and then moving on to more complex ones later, or vice versa? Author Brian Tracy answered this in his book *Eat That Frog!*[29,30] The term "Frog" symbolizes your most value-adding task that needs addressing before any other. The title refers to a saying, "If you eat a live frog at the start of the day, expect this to probably be the worst thing that will happen to you all day long." The author adds that if you must eat two frogs, then start with the ugliest one first. He derives the metaphor from the need to rank the highest value-laden activities that contribute most to your end goal. In other words, do the hard important work first.

When we develop a work plan, we are usually presented with many items to rank in terms of priority. We often tend to start with the quicker but lesser-value ones while deferring the "frog" to a later time, and the cycle repeats. We end up finding ourselves busy spending time and energy on low-value activities that are easier to accomplish. This habit contributes little to our success and limits our chances of growth, robbing us of a sense of accomplishment.

The Pareto principle states that a fraction of the total effort you exert (around 20%) can be associated with a larger portion of the desired outcome (around 80%). The highest value-adding tasks belong to that 20% category. A fraction of your planned work ends up holding more value than the remaining activities all combined. During the planning phase, you first need to carefully identify all the activities you want to complete by the end of the day. You then need to *identify the tasks that bring the highest return on your invested time and energy*. These are your high-priority items that need your utmost attention and should be addressed at the start of the day.

Prioritizing your most valuable task is an effective strategy to increase productivity even if this task is the most difficult one. Doing so will require discipline and self-control. With time, this practice will evolve into a routine. The feeling of accomplishment and success will increase your self-esteem. Thus, driving you to develop this into a habit.

As you churn through your workday, it becomes important to recognize the progress you are making, even if it may seem small. An article in the Harvard Business Review titled "The Power of Small Wins,"[31] found that progressing in meaningful work is key. Acknowledging this progress is one of the most powerful tools for boosting motivation. The more you are aware of the progress you make, the more productive you can become. *We tend to be so focused on the end goal that we ignore the small steps that get us there.* The next time you achieve an interim milestone, make the effort to recognize the small progress you have made. Do so knowing that this recognition will benefit your path towards success. Technology can assist in tracking your progress. Goal-tracking apps, for instance, display your progress and how close you are to your target. Do not forget to reward yourself in between.

One of the side effects of the COVID-19 pandemic has been an increase in the number of meetings (conducted mostly virtually) due to the loss of face-to-face communication. A 2021 Microsoft survey[32] uncovered that Teams meetings have more than doubled compared to a year earlier. We are often invited to attend unrelated meetings; these result in an efficiency reduction. By attending unnecessary meetings we spend time away from work without much benefit in return. Workers can spend up to 85% of their time in meetings.[33] The MIT Sloan Management Review describes results from companies that implemented at least one meeting-free day per week.[33] This plan resulted in a significant increase in productivity, communication, and engagement. A reduction in stress in employees was also observed. *The key takeaway is to focus on attending meetings that impact your work and career development directly and efficiently.*

When invited for a call, ask yourself how you might contribute to it and what benefits it could bring to you. Since you will be spending time away from your own tasks, try to skip (when possible) the sessions that bear little to no relevance to you. The same logic applies when you organize a meeting. Refrain from inviting those who will not add or receive value from the meeting. Prepare a clear agenda and set a time for the session to end as required. This will allow for the meeting to run as efficiently as possible. *When possible, schedule all your meetings on selected days during the week;* this will free up time for yourself and others for the rest of the workweek without meeting interruptions.

Emails are also responsible for draining our productivity. They keep coming, rendering your focus on valuable tasks difficult. You could silence your inbox notifications to avoid being distracted or schedule windows of time throughout the day to check email. This will help remove email distractions during your work. You will then have the time to read and address the email messages at the scheduled time. There are also various email settings where you can temporarily block incoming emails or mark certain emails as very important to apply notification. This will help ensure a distraction-free period. Closing your email is another way you can avoid the temptation to keep checking your inbox.

Check out the Pomodoro Technique: The Pomodoro Technique is an effective, easy to adapt, and proven time management method. Created by Francesco Cirillo,[34] the Pomodoro Technique has been used by millions globally. The method includes principles reviewed earlier, such as taking breaks and limiting interruptions. A high-level summary of the technique is provided below:

- List the tasks that need to be completed (break down complex ones into sub-components where needed).
- Set a timer for 25 minutes.
- During this window of time, focus all your energy and attention on one item and avoid interruptions.
- Once the alarm goes off, immediately stop what you are doing and take a five-minute break before starting the next task.
- Each cycle is called a Pomodoro.
- You deserve a 15 to 20 minute break after four Pomodoros.

One reason why the Pomodoro method is effective

is that it allows you to focus on your work. The Pomodoro Technique helps you avoid checking the remaining time on the clock by leaving that to the alarm you set. It changes your perception of time. Time can now be viewed as a defined, measurable, and manageable resource; thus, allowing you to live in the moment as you focus your energy on one task at a time.

Set Your State of Mind: Creating routine has a positive impact on your wellbeing. According to a study by David Eilam, PhD, establishing a routine can help manage stress and result in a calmer mind.[35] We all have different schedules and responsibilities throughout the day; the idea is to define a routine that works best for you. More importantly, stick to the plan once it is in effect.

Do not forget ergonomics. Take ergonomics seriously. Your physical setup is associated with health benefits. Productivity can also be affected by your office and desk layout. Research has shown that even your workstation setup plays an important role in your performance.[36] Keeping ergonomics in mind can help you achieve higher levels of productivity. Maintaining a good posture when working is also important as it impacts your performance.[37] Refer to Chapter Three "If These Walls Could Talk" for more information on the impact of environmental surroundings to your wellbeing and productivity.

In his book, *The Positive Dog*,[38] Jon Gordon states that a negative attitude impacts many aspects of our lives, including productivity. A positive attitude leads to success, happiness, and the development of leadership skills. *Your state of mind can be consciously altered to help you transition to a positive attitude*. Below are some ways that can help you maintain or develop a positive mindset:

- Frequent positive-minded people.
- Focus on positive thoughts.
- Be grateful for what you have.
- Be supportive of others.
- Perform good deeds.
- Spread happiness around you by smiling.
- Do not allow negative emotions to build up.

- Reward yourself by celebrating achievements, even if they are small, throughout the day.

Last but not least, even though not a specific productivity technique, it would be amiss not to conclude with how important it is to free your time by delegating tasks to others. Learning how to properly delegate is a powerful habit that can improve your productivity. We often tend to take on more work than we should and ignore that others can help share some of the load we carry. Knowing what tasks to delegate, and to whom, will help you reduce your workload. This will allow you to focus on the key activities that need your attention.

Behavioral scientist Ashley Whillans, PhD, cleverly reminded us that "outsourcing chores could make you as happy as getting an $18,000 raise."[39] There is a benefit in trading money for time. Delegating also provides opportunities to develop the younger workforce. By asking others to help you, you are empowering them and building trust. Always be specific in your expectations, provide a deadline, and ask staff to review their work before concluding it. In other words, help others help you. Under promise and over deliver. Do not burn out. Keep a healthy, positive, engaged, and productive planned approach to both your personal and professional life.

CHAPTER THREE
If These Walls Could Talk

Well, guess what? The walls are sending you a subtle message that significantly impacts your health and wellbeing, in both a physical and mental way. This is my favorite chapter because every person around me that has implemented some of these concepts has witnessed immediate gratification and renewed optimism. *Our physical space affects our mental one!* No doubt about it.

As you go through this chapter, remember that this is not about spending more money on furniture or organizing. This chapter is about intentional thoughts regarding how you want your surroundings to represent you and make you feel. *You will eliminate the heaviness of "things" that do not make you feel good.* As a result, you will highlight what makes you bright, happy, and productive.

This chapter is about making your space your happy place.

I just finished cleaning, tidying, donating, sorting, recycling...I love it. Minimalism, here I come. Yet the space and the pace of my life have not changed. I feel stuck, in a rut! Now what? There is a disconnect between my living environment and what I want for my everyday life. Do I need to buy a new house, move to a new apartment, tidy up some more? Should I quit my job? Volunteer more? Attempt a career switch? Switch college majors? Get a college minor? Why am I like this? I just want to be happy!

If you ever felt this way, do not worry, you are not alone. So what is the answer? The previous chapter on productivity shed some light on the concept. Time to expand on it. The answer is *carving space in your life that allows you to fulfill your time on the activities that make you happy and successful.* Many of these stale and anxious feelings come from disillusionment, or after major life events:

- Job loss, job change, or promotion.
- Divorce, breakup, or loneliness.
- Winning, losing, or inheriting money.
- Pregnancy and postpartum.
- Illness, injury, or recovery.
- Weight gain or loss.
- Pandemic and war fears.
- Marriage.
- Retirement.
- Grief.
- A move.

Our habitat plays a large role in dictating our behavior and vice versa. Just as in nature, our habitat can nurture specific traits and naturally select for them! The survival of the fittest. We have the choice to make our built environment, our habitat, our home, and our workplace reflect this survival and select to showcase our strength. So let us do it! Let us create this powerful infrastructure. Make room for a life change!

The minimalism movement has a strong following that surged on social media, TED Talks, and the bookshelves. I, for one, am a big fan. However, when major life events happen, or when your life needs an event to shake things up, tidying up and minimizing may only provide temporary relief and gratification. Your habitat and surrounding built spaces should always reflect the mental and physical infrastructure that leads to your success. This field of study is referred to as environmental psychology.

ENVIRONMENTAL PSYCHOLOGY PLAYS A LARGE ROLE IN YOUR WELLBEING, HAPPINESS, AND SATISFACTION

The built environment is defined as a human-made space and surroundings where you interact and spend most of your time in. For example, your home, office, and even outdoor places like parks and plazas. If you want to dive straight in and forgo the academics, go ahead and skip the next section. Just keep these principles in mind:

- Your goals will change over time. This is how growth happens. It is okay to go through this process in different ways multiple times. Much of this process is based on life events.

- This chapter is not a workbook for organization and minimalism! This is about highlighting ideas to help you engage your space to work for YOU. Your practical, efficient infrastructure that yields the things that make you happy and successful. This is not limited to home ownership. The same principles apply to a specific room in your house, or your rental apartment, a room at your parents' house, dorm, office, garden, and anywhere you interact with the physical or built environment. This could even include your car and your digital devices!

- Spending money on furniture and home organization solutions is not critical for this to be successful. You need to create "space allocation zones" and invest "thought" into your built environment.

- You can break the rules. The space needs to represent and suit you. Sometimes less is more, so go ahead and edit. More importantly, be clean and neat. Yet, sometimes bold is necessary. The flow of the space should augment your vision and thoughts. Do not be afraid to be different or loud in your ideas. As long as you stay neat and clean.

- As we delve into the emotional and mental impact of the built environment on wellbeing, we cannot undermine the impact of indoor environmental health. Whether it is noise, lighting, mold, chemical emissions, gas leaks, formaldehyde from furniture and carpets, inadequate ventilation, radon, asbestos, leaded pipes, dust, pests, pollen, or volatile organic compounds from paint, *the "sick building syndrome" manifests itself into both physical and clinical ailments.*

SOME ACADEMIC PROOF

When hearing the word "environment," one thinks of

large scale topics that involve the outdoors. For example, climate change or plastic islands floating in the oceans.

Our environment should also be viewed at a smaller local personal scale, to include our indoor surroundings. Reflecting on the health of the interior built space environments is equally important to our global wellbeing. After all, nature makes the best habitats, so we could learn a thing or two by mimicking nature!

Karakas and Yildiz used methodologies in neuroscience to better understand the human experience in the built environment while emphasizing that, "the built environment provides a habitat for the most sophisticated mammal in our universe, the human being!"[1] In this study, published in Elsevier's Frontiers of Architectural Research, the authors recorded that advances in science and technology have facilitated the measurements of psychophysiological responses. In the world of big data analyses, you have to measure to manage.[2] One of the most noteworthy conclusions in this 2020 study[1] is that: tools are now available that can measure real-time psychophysiological responses to objectively assess the influence of the built environment on humans' behavioral, sensational, emotional, and cognitive responses. *We can now go beyond the theories of environmental psychology and present evidence-based conclusions for better architectural and living spaces.*

The ability to study real-time emotional and sensory responses will continue to provide the field of environmental psychology tools to better understand the dynamic relationships between wellbeing and the built environment.

With the availability of a multitude of digital, real-time, and wearable sensors, we can measure how occupants interact with their building space in terms of energy utilization,[2] thermal and visual comfort, and indoor air quality. These sensors include but are not limited to motion, sound, photo, humidity, CO_2, volatile organic compounds, room temperature, thermal body temperature, camera, pupilometers, and heart rate monitors.

In an innovative 2018 US Environmental Protection Agency funded study,[3] investigators Joon-Ho et al. studied human-building integration by measuring occupant eye pupil changes in response to lighting control. Such studies can help building managers better understand the indoor environment, potential energy savings, and visual comfort levels of building occupants.

In July 2020, as the world battled the mental drain of the COVID-19 pandemic, the Barcelona Institute for Global Health published a randomized crossover study[4] on the physical and mental health effects of repeated short walks in different space environments. The study measured the self-reported wellbeing and mood, blood pressure, and heart rate variability of 59 healthy office workers as they were exposed to either blue space, urban space, or the control site. The study concludes significant improved wellbeing and mood responses in the blue space. Blue space usually represents either natural or anthropogenic (human-made) outdoor environments that project a blue color, such as water features or skies.

With mental health issues on the rise, it is important to pay more attention to environmental psychology and how it impacts and expedites our healing. The Barcelona Institute for Global Health study[4] is one of the newest quantitative research representing the connection between "mood" and physical surroundings in the environment. Our home is part of this physical environment we live in - whether indoors or outdoors. Yet, the acknowledgment that our emotions and wellbeing are affected by the physical environment has been around for thousands of years; more specifically, over 3000 years as Feng Shui.

Feng Shui (wind water) is defined by the Oxford dictionary[5] as a Chinese system of laws that governs spatial arrangement and orientation in relation to the flow of energy (qi), and whose favorable or unfavorable effects are considered when siting and designing buildings. Where qi, like the air we breathe, is the central underlying principle in Chinese traditional medicine and Chinese martial arts. In simplistic terms, *Feng Shui originated around 3000 years ago in China as an ancient art of placement for healthy living spaces.*

This harmony with the surroundings (Feng Shui), 3000 years later, continues to provide architectural guidelines, marketing perspectives, staging ideas, book publications, and new research opportunities.

Then comes one of the most influential artists of the 20th century, Pablo Picasso (1881-1973). Some of Picasso's most famous work demonstrated cubism, a visually abstracted artistic movement that augmented geometric shapes in depictions of humans and other forms. Some of Picasso's famous quotes include, "learn the rules like a pro so you can break them like an artist" and "art washes away from the soul the dust of everyday life."

From 3000 year old guidelines of Feng Shui to the magnificent creativity of Pablo Picasso, as different as these two movements are, they both respect how our surroundings influence our feelings.

Elsevier publications have dedicated an entire peer-reviewed journal to the scientific study of the transactions and interrelationships between people and their surroundings in the Journal of Environmental Psychology. Robert Gifford, PhD, a leading author in the Department of Psychology, University of Victoria, Canada, indicates that the number of submissions to the Journal of Environmental Psychology quadrupled from 2002 to 2012, and interest in the field has been awakened by many variables to include the realization of the ability of environmental psychology to contribute ideas and solutions to the design of the built environment. *Fueled by deteriorations in mental health, we cannot underestimate the importance of the built environment - including our homes - to one's health and wellness.*

Attachments and identity to a place happen through three concepts described by Scannel and Gifford.[6] The three concepts are people, places, and processes. For example, 1) attachment to a person or people that live in that space or community, 2) attachment to the spatial and physical dimension, and 3) a feel-good process that reminds you of positive past events or good self-esteem and pride. The second concept, place attachment, can vary in scale to multiple spatial levels. In our built environment, it can be something as simple as being attached to a chair or a neighborhood park! As Stedman,[7] 2003 explains, this spatial attachment is not merely the connection to the physical features, but to the meaning those features represent.

Perception plays a large role in how we assess our spatial environment. The 2014 published Environmental Psychology Matters[8] showed us how colors, décor, and other built variables impact how credible we see the owners of the space, how memorable the space is, or how we feel in it.

When it comes to restoring wellbeing and health, many articles have been published regarding incorporating nature into one's healing. In the indoors, Ulrich 1984,[9] Kweon et al. 2008,[10] and Raanaas et al. 2011,[11] have all published that incorporating nature into our built environment could be as simple as seeing nature through a window, or an image, or potted plants.

Ulrich 1984 studied[9] hospital records of patients

recovering from gallbladder removal surgery in a Pennsylvania hospital between 1972 and 1981. Some patients were assigned to rooms with a window view of a natural setting while others were in rooms with windows facing brick building walls. *The patients with a nature view, not only had shorter postoperative hospital stays but also received fewer pain medicines, and less negative evaluative remarks on their files from nurses.*

When windows are not an option, poster frames are a suitable alternative. Kweon et al. 2008[10] studied poster frames hung on walls in office environments! The study focused on the workplace where *one out of four American workers report themselves to be "chronically angry" and stressed.* In this study, 210 college students were assigned randomly to different office conditions where abstract and nature paintings were hung on the walls and then were later asked to perform anger-provoking computer tasks. The results concluded that males experienced less anger and stress when art posters were present, especially nature paintings. Females did not have as strong of a response. Gender and evolutionary differences in perception and anger remain where females experience and communicate stress and anger differently from males. The computer task did not seem to ignite as much anger in the females as it did in their male counterparts.

Building on work by Ulrich[9] and others, a team of cross-disciplinary experts (Connellan et al. 2013)[12] published a literature review to answer: How does the intersection of mental health care and architecture contribute to positive mental health outcomes? To address this challenge, multiple experts worked together in a team. The team included practicing architects, social scientists, psychologists, a mental health nurse professor, and a lecturer in design theory specializing in design and wellbeing. The project was mainly based in Australia and the United Kingdom. The study systemically studied 165 research articles. Based on the expertly chosen keywords, themes started emerging. Some themes overlapped and statistical correlations were used to test several ideas. These themes lead to conclusions that environmental stress, color, perceptions of safety and security in crowding, quiet rooms to seclude, garden access, natural light and lighting, interior design, spatial organization and distribution, visual therapy, and dedicated places (whether for socializing or retiring), can all influence and enhance the mental and physical wellbeing of occupants. For example, *patients in brightly lit rooms stay on average 2.6 days less in the hospital than those in dimly lit rooms.*[12, 13]

Preferences for single occupancy bedrooms and privacy were important. Interior design features including: furnishings, color, wayfinding, cognitive mapping, spatial organization, and type of patient room, dictate the need for clear visual communication balanced with a homey environment.[12,14] Meanwhile, closed nursing stations can appear inaccessible to patients and visitors.[12,15]

Even more significantly, Daykin et al.[16] showcased aesthetic therapy. *Depression and anxiety were 34% and 20% lower, respectively, when patients were exposed to arts.*[12,16]

In conclusion, studies advocate incorporating

evidence-based designs for mental wellbeing, and emphasized the importance of user input as part of the process.[12]

Another important aspect of our interaction with the built environment is productivity (see Chapter Two for more on productivity). The more productive we are, the less mentally burdened we feel. In a 2017 study, Mallawaarachchi et al.[17] quantitatively modeled this productivity effect in three selected green-rated office buildings in Sri Lanka. The study confirmed the relationship between the built environment and occupants' productivity. *Five critical factors were highlighted as statistically significant either as helpful or inverse: air quality, system control (acoustic), acoustical partitioning, amount of space, and open-plan (negative correlation).*

Do these above factors remind you of anything? The elements of light, noise, space - does that sound like nature to you? Learning from nature, bringing the indoors out and the outdoors in, produces an organic habitat feel for many. *Nature, after all, builds the best habitats. This concept is termed as biophilic design and defined in the building industry as: a method to connect occupants with the natural environment.*

Humans are inherently and intrinsically connected to natural systems and processes. This inclination not only is important for our physical and mental wellbeing, but it is also important in how we associate with other forms of life and each other.

In a 2018 study,[18] Lee and Park assessed the importance of linking people and nature in children's libraries. Lessons learned from surveying 261 caregivers include offering experiences of natural ecosystems to children. Specifically, including multifunctional natural shelter space and open designs that encourage: reading, resting, gathering, play and performance, and facilitate interaction among users. As a bonus, the natural elements induce interest through various forms of sensory experiences that are created by the biophilic designs.

Biophilic designs are not only for children. Kids are attracted and engaged by tree houses, habitat shelters, and mimicked outdoor assemblies in indoor playgrounds and libraries (example: indoor models of animals, ponds, tents, castles, treehouses, bridges, and trees). *Adults, on the other hand, are always looking for that perfect view!* In real estate, a perfect view comes with a higher price tag.

In 2019, Xue et al.[19] introduced us to important strategies in biophilic urbanism by engaging stakeholders in Singapore. The authors examined strategies that would be cost effective and favored creating biophilic infrastructure that includes green space and sensorial design. The authors concluded that decorative and ornamental elements would be the least cost effective. On the other hand, *concepts of open space, airflow, natural plants, natural landscape, natural ventilation, green space, window views of the natural landscape, and open plazas for community gatherings would be worth the investment in terms of benefit to cost ratio.* To close, as Beatley (2016) stated, "nature is not optional, but an absolutely essential quality of modern urban life."[19,20]

⊘ TRY THIS: SURROUND YOURSELF
WITH THE GOOD STUFF!

The built environment you live in and interact within reflects on your wellbeing, mood, health, and productivity. Without making any decisions, having this self-awareness can guide you to the best physical changes to accommodate better living surroundings. Physical changes can happen all at once or in small steps, one at a time. The reorganization can happen in one area or multiple areas. The adjustments can happen in large living spaces or small ones. Even virtually sorting and cleaning your inbox, files, and smart apps can feel great and save you time in the long run. Remember your space, your rules! Just keep your changes conducive and productive to your needs and desires for that space.

The following are a few ideas that you can begin to implement. Before you start:

Safety First: Start on a clean slate. Make sure your

indoor environment is pollutant free, clean of molds, dust, strong odors or perfumes, tripping hazards, and any other factor that could pose a safety concern. If you need to hire professionals, the expense is well justified. Do not attempt to "fix" things in trades that you have no working knowledge of. Keep your home well ventilated by circulating indoor air out and bringing outdoor air in. Open your windows and doors occasionally to circulate the air in your home despite the weather. Make sure your room temperatures are set to a comfortable level. Check the ergonomics of your desk chairs and driving seat, and make sure your bed/pillows are comfortable for a sound sleep.

If all is safe and clear, give your space a good deep cleaning. Put away that laundry that has been piling on. Sort the mail that has been accumulating. Clean your car (yes, your car that you spend enough time in can significantly influence your mood). The fun stuff is yet to come, but first, let us start on a safe and clean slate!

Music: The Greek philosopher, Plato, said that "music and harmony find their way into the inward places of the soul." Make sure that music finds its place in your home and life as well. There is an indescribable feeling when music truly understands your sadness, sparks your motivation, and expresses your inner thoughts. So use music to elevate your mood and enhance the task at hand. Choose the correct music for the ambiance you want to experience. Use music to shield you from a noisy environment. Of course, use caution by wearing earphones safely (especially if you are not sitting indoors) and be mindful of others around you.

Brighter Rooms, Brighter You (Phototherapy/Light Therapy): Sometimes used for Seasonal Affective Disorder (SAD), Light Therapy/Phototherapy is linked to many benefits such as eliminating fatigue, increasing focus, regulating sleep patterns, and elevating mood. Also known as the "window healing effect," this therapy is not only about viewing nature, but also about bringing more light into the room to enhance the occupants' mood.

Incorporating nature and light into our built environment could be as simple as seeing nature through a window, or an image (wall art), large mirrors, and dramatic light fixtures. Even in rental properties or dorm rooms, you can easily use large floor lamps and safely lean wall mirrors to better reflect light in your surroundings. This could all be accomplished without construction damage or changing the paint colors on the walls.

Biophilic Design: Bio (biology/life) philic (tendency), literally translates to the inherent human tendency of leaning towards the natural environment and elements. Thus, the term biophilic design. Biophilic design aims to connect occupants with their natural environment through design concepts. These concepts depend on natural lighting and landscaping, open ventilation, potted plants, and the use of various elements such as wood, clay, wool, metal, leather, stones, and textured organic fabrics and materials.

In Canada, doctors write "a prescription for nature"

through the PaRX Program that launched in November 2020.[21] Participating doctors prescribe sun, visits to park trails, and fresh air for their patients. These "Park Prescriptions"[22] started as a grassroots movement in the United States to promote physicians prescribing park activity for better health outcomes. *Standard recommendations include two hours in nature per week, at a minimum of twenty minutes each time.* The healing power of nature can impact mental and physical health, including high blood pressure, diabetes, focus, anxiety, and depression. Sun exposure also alleviates vitamin D deficiency that is found in many communities. This deficiency is linked with lower immunity and feelings of sadness.

Learn from nature to create an organic habitat feel. As I said before, nature makes the best habitats. Try to bring the outdoors in and indoors out. Use or simulate earthy elements in your surroundings and fabrics for a biophilic effect in your space.

Find organic textures in pillows, throws, curtains, furniture, clay pots, wicker or metal baskets, and window coverings that evoke a natural element in your home.

Art and Expression (Aesthetic Therapy): Art, paintings, prints, and photographs have been documented to enhance occupants' temperament in rooms. This is why you find artwork in hotels and hospitals. Your house should include larger pieces that have meaning to you. They do not need to be expensive. You can even attempt painting them or framing prints of photos you took.

Wall art, poster frames, blown up photos, paintings, and drawings can make a unique statement and set the right mood in a room. Express yourself. Usually larger pieces make a bigger impact and look less cluttered.

You do not have to spend too much money on your statement piece. Commission a local artist or do it yourself with the help of a talented loved one. Look up free ideas and tutorials online. Search "textured paint art" or "poured paint art," "furnisher makeovers," or spend a Saturday morning creating your own photoshoot of your favorite natural/urban spot in town. The theme could be pop artsy or from nature, classic, modern, or abstract. The colors can be muted, black and white, or colorful! Use your favorite colors, get creative and enjoy the process. You can always change your mind and use a fresh piece or exchange the artwork every season. Go ahead and try it!

Furnishing, Signaling, and Wayfinding: Visual communications through interior design features can signal how to best use a space. For example, furniture placement allows us to use a dining room as an office by placing a desk there. There is no cookie-cutter, correct, or wrong way on how one should use and furnish a space in a home.

Spending money on furniture and home organization solutions is not critical for this to be successful. You need to invest "space allocation zones" and "thought" into your built environment. In other words, ask yourself: how do I want to use this space? How will this space better serve my needs?

We are accustomed to placing certain furniture

pieces in specific rooms. What works for one family does not work for another. You can turn your formal dining room into an office, or turn your office into a playroom. It is okay to turn your breakfast nook into a gardening station where you sort and pot your seeds, especially in severe weather. It is okay to turn your guest room into a home gym or home office. There are many ways you can incorporate multifunctional room designs, especially given the modular furnishing ideas available on the market. How about a writing desk in lieu of your night table? Some of the best authors produced their work from their bedrooms. Allocate space for what works for you.

You can break the rules. The space needs to represent and suit you. Sometimes less is more, so edit. More importantly, be clean and neat. You can be clean and neat while also being bold and impactful. The flow of the space should augment your vision and thoughts. Do not be afraid to be different or loud in your ideas.

Decorative items (if not utilitarian, functional, and practical) are best removed from surfaces. Unless decorative items have a historical or personal value, you are best using the empty surfaces for more actionable purposes.

Wayfinding is commonly used in business spaces such as academia, libraries, hospitals, and large business centers. The main objective of wayfinding is to create an identity and location guide for each space. Signage and orientation cues are used to accomplish the goal of leading the occupant to the specific location and its uses. Visual characters are usually unique to support the purpose of each room. For example, in student unions, colorful sofas and modular tables are used to encourage the students to gather and work together or eat a to-go meal while socializing with their classmates and friends. These visual cues can also be used in your home space to invite conversation, productivity, coffee time, meditation, gathering for a meal, or whatever purpose you want your set place to represent.

With mental health issues on the rise, it is important to be mindful of environmental psychology and how it impacts and expedites our healing. This mindfulness is not based on just a book. It is based on how the space makes you feel. So remember, your space, your good feels!

CHAPTER FOUR
I Wish I Were Special

Do you ever look up to someone and get completely drawn to their charisma? It is not just about how they look. As the French say, that "*je ne sais quoi,*" that unnamed quality. Something about this person just makes you want to do more. Maybe it inspires you to dress better or speak more eloquently. Is their presence attractive? When they walk into a room, are all eyes drawn to them?

Do you know what this is called? This attractive and charismatic presence is called "confidence!" This chapter is about giving you the confidence to market your brand. Your personal brand, not your social media presence, nor your professional expertise; that all follows. Why does a personal brand matter? Your personal brand is important for your character and reputation formation. *Your reputation is critical in both your personal and professional dealings.* Reputation formation is built through time as a result of direct experiences.[1] In an interesting perspective, a 2021 study describes reputation and honest signaling as "the language of cooperation."[2] The authors write that the field of reputation forming is very complex and we are only in the initial stages of understanding it in the context of social and behavioral norms, gossip, and other frameworks. Many of the studies have not even approached reputation forming through social media interactions.

Who best to form your reputation and market your brand better than to do it yourself! You should know yourself and your aspirations best. So trust in your capabilities and let me break it down for you.

CONFIDENCE IS A MULTIFACETED TRAIT

Many factors (genetic, upbringing, and environmental) contribute to developing confidence. The basic infrastructure of confidence, self-esteem, can be nurtured and expanded. Do not confuse task specific confidence and self-esteem. *One can have confidence in a task or area yet have generally low self-esteem (self-worth).* In this chapter, as I write about confidence, I am writing about self-confidence, not just confidence in a specific situation. For self-confidence to happen, you have to be in control of your self-esteem as well. You have to believe in yourself.

Self-esteem impacts how we view ourselves and interact with others around us. Self-esteem also affects our decision making process. Chapter One helped us better understand ourselves and how we relate to each other, while Chapter Two promoted a focused and efficient structure in our lives. Those two chapters will ignite confidence within you because they improve your performance (confidence in tasks completed) and communication (self-assurance in dealing with others). Chapter One also provided you with the tools to acknowledge people's experiences and troubles. *Your empathy will promote an aura of kindness that others will find very endearing and comforting, and you will be more charismatic and giving.* Your warmth and acceptance will be offered even to people who do not know you well. This endearing quality signals leadership and trust in you.

This chapter will further exude your confidence by packaging your unique brand in a secure and comfortable way. So let us break down the attributes of confidence from the very beginning.

In a long-term study[3] of 8,711 children ages 0-6 years, enrolled by their mothers, the following conditions attributed to higher or lower self-esteem in the study subjects' early adulthood:

- Warm and present parenting.
- Parental relationship and presence, especially of the father role.
- A safe and organized physical environment (check out Chapter Three in this book), and

- Cognitive stimulation. All contributed to higher self-esteem. While,
- Maternal depression, and
- Poverty, contributed to lower self-esteem.

Even though the home environment in early childhood is a key influence on the development of self-esteem,[3] self-esteem and self-worth are not only constructed in early childhood.[4] In a 2014 study, three main conclusions were determined: 1) Self-esteem increases from youth to middle age and peaks at approximately 50 to 60 years, only to decrease rapidly into old age. 2) Even though self-esteem is a stable trait, it is also malleable over time, where one can go from low to high self-esteem and vice versa. 3) High self-esteem predicts success in many aspects in life, such as professional, personal, and health outcomes.[4]

Given how important self-esteem is to wellbeing overall, the process of developing self-esteem is critical for both the individual and society in general.

My favorite gift to give college graduates always included a book for them to start off their career and life journey. A book that always generated a reaction and great feedback from my recent graduates was *Strengths Finder 2.0* by Tom Rath.[5] The book takes the reader through a unique assessment, "The Clifton Strengths,"[6] and teaches the reader positive adjectives to describe themselves from the assessment results. The Clifton Strengths assessment was created by an educational psychologist, Donald Clifton, to identify traits that made top performers stand out.

My graduates used the matched adjectives from their Strengths Finder in their resumes and job interviews. *Instead of focusing on what they did not have (the zero to two years of experience) they focused on their strengths that would be an asset to the employer.*

Something as simple as this gift from their professor, who believed in them, provided my students vital confidence in their early adulthood and carried through as they gained more experience in their field of study.

Birth order is another important aspect to be aware of regarding personality traits, including confidence.

Multiple studies in the United States have associated high self-esteem with firstborns/only children[7,8] and lower self-esteem with middle born children.[9] Yet, in a comprehensive 2021 study in Frontiers in Psychiatry,[10] Fukuya et al. investigated birth order and various mental health variables in Japan. Interestingly, Fukuya et al.'s study demonstrated that the lowest "happiness" score was found in middle born children, while the self-esteem score was not associated with birth order in the young elementary school subjects. The study highlights that *it is important to differentiate age and cultural variations when investigating mental health variables of self-esteem, happiness, resilience, and social skills.*

Different cultures have "school transitions" and the stress exposure that comes with it at different ages. Different cultures have unique sociocultural characteristics that affect childrearing. In some cultures, firstborns are more likely to be subjected to stricter upbringing and more responsibility to take care of their younger siblings and the household, whereas lastborns are raised laxer and have both parents and older siblings to depend on. Childrearing influences self-esteem and confidence.

Cultures also differ in childrearing practices. In some cultures, parents prioritize physical proximity to their children while others prefer to give children the tools to be more independent and autonomous.[10] There is no right or wrong cookie-cutter approach when it comes to birth order and childrearing practices. However, research continues to dissect the relationship between these factors to self-esteem in various chapters of one's life. Even having sisters versus brothers as siblings can impact the dynamics of birth order. The age gap among siblings could also be another influence on birth order traits. More research is needed to find comprehensive solutions addressing the influence of birth order on self-esteem.

Beyond birth order, early childhood, and early adulthood, confidence is important for healthy personal and romantic relationships. Dr. Aaron Ben-Ze'ev, a leading expert in the study of emotions, describes qualities of high self-esteem in relationships to include: self-acceptance, calmness, humility, generosity, gratitude and a lack of feeling superior to others (i.e., no constant comparison with others). He also emphasizes that individuals with high self-esteem are more independent yet form a deeper bond in the relationship and their relationship is more stable. On the other hand, relationships based on low self-esteem are plagued by jealousy, insecurity, hostility, conflict, fear of rejection, pessimism, and are overall low quality.[11]

Different genders relate to being confident in different ways. For example, studies show that women can be less confident than men. Confidence in women is so critical that it is equally important to actual competence for success.[12] Women tend to underestimate themselves more. They have more self-doubt; they take fewer risks and ask for lower salaries. Women can also feel like a "fraud" in their accomplishments. We talk more about imposter syndrome at the end of this chapter. The gap in confidence between men and women stems from multiple factors, to include biology and upbringing.[12] Meanwhile, studies show that men can overestimate their abilities.

Even when men doubt themselves, they do not allow their feelings to hinder their actions.[12] People can "honestly" be overconfident. I write "honestly" because overconfident people truly believe in their capabilities. Overconfidence differs from narcissism. Overconfident people truly believe in themselves and come across as admirable and likable. Women tend to hold themselves back, especially from making a contradictory point or speaking out loud because of cultural and background stigmas. When men speak out loud, their opinions are regarded as part of their leadership.

Despite variation in confidence, it is good to know that confidence is an acquired trait that anyone can practice. For women, encouragement usually plays a critical role in allowing them to have that self-reassurance to build on self-confidence and task specific confidence.

COMPARISON IS THE THIEF OF JOY

Theodore Roosevelt said that "comparison is the thief of joy." Mark Twain emphasized that "comparison is the death of joy." I remind you that this journey is about your evolution, not anybody else's. Do not allow anyone to steal your joy, not even your own self-defeating thoughts. We tend to be our biggest critic, which is not always a good thing.

The same way you see others at their best, see yourself at your highest potential. Do not compare where you are in your life to other people's lives or experiences. We all go through ups and downs. *Adulthood really is acknowledging and riding the high and low waves of life gracefully.* When you are on a high, stay humble and be grateful. When life tumbles you down, know that there is always tomorrow - or the day after, the month after, the year after... Stay hopeful, positive, and consistent in your upward trajectory (Chapter One). No matter what, practice gratitude. On any given day, there is someone dealing with a rougher time than you.

Comparing yourself to others is emotionally exhausting and will only exacerbate your insecurities. Insecurity can be linked to many reasons and past life experiences. For example:

- Negative childhood experiences such as overly critical parents, abandonment issues, neglect, and even abuse.

- Always trying to compare and measure up to others - social media makes it easier to fall in this trap. Just remember we post what we want people to see. Our social media posts do not reflect all aspects of our lives, good or bad.

- Being a perfectionist - always. This behavior adds much stress and anxiety because nobody is perfect.

- You are not able to cope with failure and rejection.[13] Surround yourself with positive and supportive people. Sometimes we have to fail to reach our highest potential. How we recover from mistakes and what we learn from them is what differentiates us (See Chapter One for more on resiliency).

Some insecurity is normal. Insecurity may even motivate us to push ourselves further. Just be mindful when you get absorbed in these negative thoughts. When you get entangled in these self-defeating thoughts, adjust course and mend the root cause of your self-doubt and insecurity. Be mindful of your triggers.

I remind you again, in this journey, you are not alone in these feelings.

CONFIDENCE AND ANXIETY

Building confidence can help with anxiety. "Confident people tend to disregard whatever symptoms of anxiety they experience, focusing instead on moving forward in their task-directed efforts."[14] As an example, students' math anxiety could improve by boosting confidence and lowering stress around the topic.[15] Even in professional sports, confidence plays a large role in reducing nerves during important game moments. This is why many professional sports teams have on-staff sports psychologists to assist with building up confidence and calming nerves. Especially in away games, there were higher correlations between anxiety and lower confidence.[16] This trend acknowledges the importance of mental health and mental strength on the impact of athletes' performance.

Later on in the chapter, we mention the Action-Sentence Compatibility Effect and how cheering someone on could be beneficial. Same with confidence building. Sometimes all we need is this little extra push and encouragement. So surround yourself with supportive people and avoid toxic people that bring you down (Chapter One).

In a 2021 University of California Santa Cruz study,[17] the authors measured the effects of meeting initially by text versus video and how that impacts confidence and performance. Interestingly enough, the test subjects that first met via text messages were more confident in their interaction compared to people that met by video chat first. The study concludes that "how people first get to know each other impacts how they feel about their conversations and how effectively they work together."[17]

Audiovisual cues are important in communication. Face-to-face communication remains the most efficient form of connecting with others. Yet, the initial text messages increased confidence at the beginning of the relationship to allow for smoother interaction. The test subjects described their conversations as "more personal and natural"[17] when they text messaged before they video chatted. Online dating seems to work the same way. Many couples get to know each other through text messaging before building the confidence to talk, video chat, or meet face-to-face. Text messages can hide the awkwardness and shyness in our voice vocals and body cues. They can even mask many other emotions.

All in all, first impressions, reputation formation, stress, character, risk taking, upbringing, culture, gender, birth order, and many other aspects are related to confidence and self-esteem. Despite all these variations, one aspect remains the same: *confidence building is a learned behavior*. The following section will allow us to better practice confidence building.

⊘ TRY THIS: BUILD A CONSISTENT BRAND FOR YOURSELF!

Fulfilling our own needs by being a source of happiness from within will only nurture our relationships. Like the common adage, *"you have to be able to love yourself first."*

Clothing, vocabulary, and upkeep are not the all-in-all, but they all matter. When interacting with others, do not talk about or boast about yourself. This is not about being egotistical. Let others notice the changes organically. Not if, but when, you get a compliment or someone notices your efforts, just smile and say "thank you." So let us have an inside out, outside in makeover. First things first:

Go to that Annual Check Up: During the pandemic, many of us skipped and delayed annual routine health, vision, and dental checkups. As applicable, get the mammogram you have been putting off or schedule that colonoscopy. Stay on top of preventive medicine. This is the time to check routine exams off your list. What does this have to do with your new brand and self-confidence? You have to be healthy on the inside so you can be healthy on the outside.

Blood work results can give insight into your immunity, energy levels, fatigue, and mood. Talk to your doctor and make sure that you get a comprehensive blood test to include vitamin D, which is not always considered routine! Many doctors are now "functional medicine" MDs. The root of many health and wellness problems can be attributed to the bearings of lifestyle, genetics, and our biochemical system.

Our diet is SAD. The Standard American Diet (SAD) lacks many nutritional elements and is overtaken by what is called empty calories. Empty calories are calories with no nutritional value, such as chips, candy, cakes, and soft drinks. According to the United States Centers for Disease Control and Prevention (CDC)[18] Vitamin B6, iron (mainly in women), and vitamin D are the three nutrients assessed with the highest prevalence of deficiency. These deficiencies vary by gender, age, and ethnicity.

Even our soils are depleted from nutrients as a result of commercial farming practices, overuse, and flooding runoff. Low levels of minerals in the body, such as magnesium, have been associated with fatigue, anxiety, and depression. Magnesium deficiency is emerging as "an alarming problem for plant and human health."[19] So take that first simple step and enhance your body's consumption of nutrients through proper diet and medical guidance. Nutrients impact not only our physical wellbeing but also our mood, mental focus, energy, and our endocrine (hormone) system.

Beyond diet, mega dosing is not always the answer to nutritional deficiencies, this is why proper blood work and monitoring by a health care provider is key. Just like prescription medication, over-the-counter supplements can cause side effects including headaches, nausea, gastrointestinal issues, and even an allergic type reaction. As an example, for some consumers, certain B type vitamins, such as B12 and even Biotin (especially in mega doses), are associated with acne breakouts. Sometimes a daily combined multivitamin/multimineral supplement is more practical and sufficient. Mega dosing should only be used when there is a medically identified deficiency that needs to be corrected.

Exercise Your Confidence: Yes, literally workout. Not just physically, but also socially. No, you are not working out to control your weight, build muscles, and look fit (though this could be a welcomed side effect). Exercising has a significant impact on your mental wellbeing, especially in the outdoors, as we described in Chapter Three. So boost your confidence by relieving your mental load simply as you are walking and sweating outside.

The second form of exercise is a social workout. The following chapter in this book can help you exercise your comfort zone by engaging socially. Build your confidence by going out of your comfort zone and socializing. Confidence needs practice. Protecting our feelings by staying at home away from people will not allow us the room to grow and exercise our social confidence. Not all interactions will be pleasant, but you will learn to grow through them and pick wisely.

For productive and confident living, we have to be willing to try newly learned skills. Stanford professor of psychology, Dr. Carol Dweck, describes how a "growth" mindset (open mindset) and the ability and willingness to develop is a great indicator of success and achievement.[20] After all, confidence is about believing in your ability to get things done, whether it is a task at hand, applying for a new job after multiple rejection, or even asking someone out.

Do not be afraid of failure. Dust yourself off and expand your abilities as you build up your life skills and confidence.

New Me, New Look: Celebrate the progress you are making by putting together a new look for yourself. The changes can be minor or remarkable, but make sure you stay consistent with the brand you want to establish for yourself.

Outfits reflect how we are perceived and how we perceive ourselves. For example, *ever notice how when you look at a firefighter in uniform, you think this person must be strong and fit*. When you look at a person wearing a white laboratory coat, do you assume that this person is smart and successful?

The way we project ourselves through clothing is very important, not just for how people see us, but also how we feel about ourselves. *Remember, what you look like on the outside is the projection you want to convey.* A decisive and generous spirit is what makes a lovable leader. Even the simplest cleanest looks can be the most attractive. This new look or really "outlook" does not have to be complicated and expensive. Your style has to be put together and thoughtful to project your attractive inner strength and kindness. You can be strong yet kind, confident yet down to earth, private yet relatable. All these qualities, as long as you are self-assured, are very attractive and charismatic.

If you do not know where to start in putting together this new "look" or brand for yourself, start by creating outfits from your favorite store. No, you do not need to spend thousands of dollars on new clothing. Window shop in person or online at a specific store you admire and see how they put the outfits together. Make an effort to recreate this look from your closet. Be consistent. Emulate looks you find attractive. These looks can be inspired by many of the curated personalized styling services you find on social media. They create outfits daily and seasonally that you can purchase through membership, or simply browse online. This effort does not have to be expensive, but it requires attentiveness.

Many successful people create an attractive capsule wardrobe filled with only a few staple pieces that they mix and match. There are many inspirations online by a simple search of "how to create a capsule wardrobe." If you are a visual person, search these keywords and click the images tab. A capsule wardrobe consists of interchangeable clothing. This reduces excessive shopping and creates a put together thoughtful look for most of your occasions. Try it!

Simplify Simplify Simplify: Simplify your eating and routine habits (for example, getting dressed in the morning or eating the same nutritional breakfast daily, or the exact same healthy lunch twice a week). Showing consistency can promote healthy eating habits and efficiency in your daily routine. This sends a mental signal of gratification, instant reward, and satisfaction. A simplified routine is a happier, more productive, and more confident you.

You Are Your Toughest Critic: Speak kindly of yourself. Do not use derogatory words when jokingly describing yourself. For example, "I am so stupid, I messed up on this again" or "I am not smart I do not understand this" or "Ugh I wish I was pretty like you,

I could never wear this." I hear people make statements like this all the time, and it really saddens me. It makes me want to reach out and say to them, "you are pretty, you are smart, stop putting yourself down!"

Starting this moment, make a promise to yourself that you will not use negative language to describe yourself. Sure, we all make mistakes and have to own and apologize for them. Sure, we do not always look good in all outfits. However, there is no need for us, ever, to use words like "stupid," "ugly," or any other undesirable term to describe ourselves or anyone else. If you have children, imagine the message you are sending to them if they hear you describe yourself in a derogatory fashion. Stop excessively apologizing by saying "I am sorry" for instances you do not need to apologize for.

Describe yourself in a positive and affirmative way, period.

Lift Your Head Up, Literally and Figuratively: Posture is very important not only from a physical health perspective but also from a mental health one. Proper posture improves circulation, airflow, and nerve and muscle alignment issues. Good posture also exudes confidence and reduces tension in the body. Social psychologist Amy Cuddy, PhD presented one of my favorite TED Talks "Your body language may shape who you are."[21]

Nonverbals govern how people feel about us and ourselves. Dr. Cuddy presented evidence, through clinical saliva sampling, on how our body chemistry changes based on our nonverbal gestures. She proved that nonverbals govern how we feel about ourselves and could change our lives meaningfully over time. Effects studied included changes in hormone chemistry such as testosterone and cortisol.[22]

For years, I encouraged my students to watch this TED Talk.[18] We also practiced "power poses" as a pep talk before my students entered important presentations, such as their thesis and dissertation defense. High power poses include chin up and hands up in a V position (the type of intrinsic pose a winner does when crossing a finish line). Other poses include the Wonder Woman pose with hands on the hips standing up tall. Posture matters. Be aware of it! Stand tall and start practicing right now.

Practice that Elevator Speech: "*Your passion is contagious.*" This was my favorite feedback from student surveys at the end of the year. Do you work in a field you love? If not, maybe it is time to reconsider. It is important to find aspects of your daily life you enjoy. However, do not go quitting your job without preparation and confidently landing another one. Meanwhile, make the time outside your paying work hours to set up a business, nurture new skills, or complete additional education. Learn more about what you can successfully switch to as a new fulfilling career.

If not your job, do you have a hobby you are passionate about? Do you collect coins? Does each coin have a story? Do you build sand castles? Nurture an herb garden and can describe how these herbs are used? Do you lead a small group at your church? Are you a youth soccer coach on the weekends? *Who are you as a professional and as a person*? Can you answer this question depending on who your audience is on an elevator ride of about 30 to 60 seconds? If not, practice, practice, and practice. This will build your self-confidence and acknowledge your unique and amazing traits that are hidden, not only from the rest of the world, but also from yourself.

This is not a simple task. You will realize that you have many positive and interesting self attributes, that it is difficult to recite them out loud in less than a minute. Enjoy the process and use powerful and positive adjectives that you very much deserve. If you find the process difficult, mainly because you are too shy, ask a trusted colleague or a close relative or friend to help you "write a bio." You will be humbled and happy to know how highly others think of you. Remember, what you might perceive as a weakness might actually be your "strengths finder!"[5,6] So choose your adjectives accordingly, in a positive manner.

Vocabulary and Voice Tone: Making a good first

impression is not just about looks, it is also about words. It is not just what you say; it is also how you say it. In Chapter One, we covered techniques to be patient and poised in communicating especially during conflict. This is important for conflict resolution, to be better understood, and to decrease your stress and anger levels.

Proper communication techniques are also critical for how you project yourself to the world around you. Does that mean go memorize all the big words in the dictionary? You can, if you like, but that is not the point. So what makes one a charismatic speaker with a confident presence?

A 2017 Yale study correlated voice and vocals to how people are perceived, believed, liked, and trusted.[22,23] This is especially applicable in today's society, where the majority of our communication is supported by audio messages and virtual calls.

In presentations, and when we initially encounter each other, our voice is most nervous in the very first words. Even a "hello" can seem shaky and out of breath. So lower your tone and speak in a calm and relaxed manner. Think back to your childhood. A parent just saying one word, your name, could tell you if they were happy or if you were in trouble! Simply put, *your mood also influences your voice, and people can notice it.* For example, have you ever answered the phone and the caller asked you if you were okay based on your voice tone? Your emotions are also heard and people pick up on them in a positive or negative way.

Unless it is a sad circumstance, when you talk in your daily life, as applicable, focus on happy thoughts with good energy. Project a powerful presence. Reject feelings of nervousness, anger, and sadness to shield your audience from your negative emotions. Exercise a steady, moderately fast (about 200 words per minute)[23] and likable positive voice projection. It shows confidence.

There are various situations that require more seriousness and empathy in your voice. Just being aware of how you are projecting through your vocals in various circumstances will make you more confident and in control of your setting.

Now that we have our voice tone under control, what about our choice of words, our vocabulary? Words have meaning and impact. *Just one word can make a difference by triggering a multitude of feelings within you and others.* A good example is a 2018 study in the Journal of Childhood Obesity. Even though the intent of the parent is to support their child in their weight loss journey; parental "weight talk" needs to be measured very carefully to prevent inducing sadness, embarrassment, and shame in their kids.[24] The parents should focus on promoting a supportive environment for the adolescents and lead by example in pursuing a healthier lifestyle.

The Cleveland Clinic Journal of Medicine offers another example of "words matter."[25] The clinical case study highlights that choice of words can sway how medical personnel assess patient dealings. More specifically, the author describes how patient history bias, for example alcoholism, may influence how laboratory tests are ordered and interpreted by a physician.[25]

On another level, word choices can impact

physical movements - not just emotional ones. A recent 2021 study demonstrates how test subjects exposed to adverbs such as "fast" and "quick" promoted physical response known as the Action-Sentence Compatibility Effect.[26] So go ahead parents, fans, and supporters, your cheers are helpful! Just pick your adverbs accordingly.

How you come across is important, and it is not just about looks and posture. Keep that in mind and chose your words and vocals accordingly.

Beware of Imposter Syndrome: Imposter syndrome is a psychological phenomenon where even highly accomplished people can feel inadequate, incompetent, or a fraud in their achievements. The syndrome is associated with low self-confidence and low self-esteem and can impede performance in many professions, to include the medical field.[27] Professionals who experience this imposter syndrome often inwardly doubt their performance despite evidence of their skills and successful contributions; they are afraid of taking any risks that could expose them.

A 2020 paper revealed that feelings of imposter syndrome can be up to 82% prevalence among individuals in the studied literature.[28] In earlier research on this topic, much of the focus was on high achieving women. Today, the statistics are also prominent among people with underrepresented identities in the workforce.

It is normal, especially when employees care so much about their work, that they double and triple-check themselves when making important decisions. In many instances, we have all felt the need for that extra "fake it till you make it" self-talk to complete an assignment or perform successfully. Minor self-doubt to help us grow is reasonable. Conversely, it is important to counter negative thoughts that impede our progress and confidence.

According to the APA[29] the following steps will help tame imposter thoughts: 1) cognitive awareness of this phenomenon that many also experience, 2) talking about these imposter feelings with trusted others who can relate 3) sharing experiences of failure with peers (or online groups) who go through the same processes, 4) celebrating and reflecting on successful milestones, 5) breaking free from the ideology of perfectionism, 6) self-compassion and 7) acknowledging and accepting these feelings when they peek through, especially in specific circumstances or during career or life changes. We can put into practice many of these steps by giving grace to ourselves and following the recommendations detailed in Chapter One. At the end of the day, confidence (like self-doubt) is highly influenced by your emotional quotient and resilience.

You are special, I hope you see it by now. Visualize the changes you are implementing to boost your self-confidence. *Just because your upbringing and experiences did not build up your self-esteem and self-confidence, it does not mean you cannot bring them out from within.* It takes hard work to build confidence to establish a brand for yourself. Believe in the process and invest time in improving specific skill sets. Confidence is a learned behavior.[30] So start by eliminating your own self-doubt and focus instead on being an active participant in conversations and interactions with others.[31] Ask questions and engage. The next chapter will guide you. I hope you give yourself a chance to highlight who you are by giving this chapter's recommendations a try.

CHAPTER FIVE
The Life of the Party

This is the fastest chapter to read, yet the most challenging because you have to put yourself out there!

Just because we are not all extroverts does not mean that we cannot be engaged in society. There is a self-conscious person in all of us. Especially post pandemic as working, studying, and socializing habits became more isolating. We became notably less interactive. *As we try to "get back at it," everything feels so chaotic.* This includes driving, eating out, interacting with the service industry, and dealing with each other. Even though it is tempting, do not retreat permanently to your shell. Solo breaks will remain critical for our wellbeing, and no, you do not have to be the life of the party. However, you need to socialize.

This chapter is about socializing you and creating a community infrastructure around you. As an introvert, nothing scares me more. Yet, *there is a value in our interactions for self-growth*. We cannot live and work alone on an island (I know some of us have tried). Being isolated reduces our exposure to new ideas, progress, and the breadth of our emotional quotient.

IT TAKES A VILLAGE

It takes a village they say - to raise a kid. What about you? Where is your village? Your backup? The infrastructure of your social being? Your community? Your neighbors? Your relatives and friends? The people that have your back and keep an eye on your wellbeing?

I remember when I was very young visiting my father's village. The village is tucked in a small Mediterranean chaparral. If you looked up, you saw mountains. If you looked down, you saw the sea. When the war erupted, the families rapidly ran over to the neighborhood church. The church was built stone by stone to house the prayers of the community. I always thought how beautiful it was that the church key was in the custody of the adjacent neighbor's home. In times of hardship, the villagers could always depend on each other. Where is our village now? Our communities are way too large to expect the same experience as a small town. Somehow, though, we should create this supportive system.

It is becoming harder and harder to be part of a community. Many of us live in large metropolitan areas. There is traffic and distance and moves due to work or military relocation. So where can we find our people? We stay connected, digitally with people that mean a lot to us, even if they are thousands of miles away. No one can replace family and friends that life keeps us apart from. However, we still need that local societal connection in our own place we call home. We have to find home, no matter where we live. *Do not be lonely and do not get used to being alone.*

SOCIALIZATION BUILDS OUR CHARACTER

Without socialization, we cannot develop the set of values, attitudes, beliefs, and behaviors associated with being one's self. This is especially important in early childhood. In other words, socialization is how we learn to develop our character.

The famous Harlow studies[1,2,3] on socialization demonstrated that isolated monkeys later became more withdrawn, hostile, and apathetic in adulthood. One study was titled "The development of learning in the rhesus monkey."[1] Notice the title included "learning," because learning is what we acquire from each other, in good and in bad.

Harry F. Harlow, PhD (1905-1981) is an American

psychologist who invested his career studying dependency needs, maternal attachment, and social isolation through the behaviors of rhesus monkeys. Harlow's theory expands on "tactile comfort" (comfort by touch/contact) in mother-infant relationships. He describes the need for contact comfort as innate (biological) within us. Dr. Harlow highlights the importance of touch, which many have lost during the recent isolating pandemic.

Harlow's experimental techniques using monkeys include depriving methods of separating infant monkeys in chambers. These methods are very difficult for me to read. Some of the cruelty and emotional damage of isolation can be healed by nurturing, especially if the void was not formed early in life. These experiments proved many theories on the importance of socialization, maternal attachment, and the innate need to stay in touch. Later on, the field developed to learn more about healthy attachments versus attachment disorders. Dr. Harlow received many awards for the advancement of psychology. Yet, his research methods remain some of the most controversial and harsh.

We have come a long way in the ethical determination of research methodology. Yet one value remains the same. *Interpersonal relationships are the infrastructure of our wellbeing in society.* Societal relationships keep us functioning as part of a physical and emotional ecosystem. We cannot live in a box alone.

A featured article in APA's Monitor on Psychology[4] calls for strong relationships as a critical public health priority. The title of this research based article is "Life-saving relationships."[4] Close emotional connections are beneficial for your health and wellness. Cumulatively, good relationships can give us a better and longer life. Recent research has even seen significant benefits of close relationships on heart disease, cancer, depression, and addiction. "It's not an exaggeration to say that lack of social connections can be deadly. Strong social relationships increase the likelihood of survival by 50 percent regardless of age, sex or health status"[4,5] according to Dr. Holt-Lunstad et al. (2010).

If you feel lonely and disconnected, you are not alone. The nation's social network has been declining over the years.[6] More specifically, we have fewer people in our lives that we can depend on for important matters. The fault should not be grossly directed at technology.[6] On the contrary, communication technologies can enhance our participation instead of sending us into further isolation. *Maybe we are too busy, burned out and unbalanced, and need to reprioritize our time and relationships.*

This feeling of isolation is not limited to single people. Even married individuals find themselves in discordant relationships.[4,7] Do not feel like you are not loved or that you do not belong. Know that many of us are facing these same challenges. This is especially obvious in the last couple of years when many were even physically isolated due to the pandemic. Moreover, the last couple of years have been especially difficult when you consider the extreme rift among social and political viewpoints. Many decided simply not to engage with each other to avoid conflict - rightfully so. But we need to do something about this lonely culture we are creating. We cannot continue the disconnect. We can interact and care for each other, even if we have different viewpoints and concerns. We need to give, mentor, lead, and encourage each other. This is how we grow and live meaningful lives. *We cannot be just another statistic on burnout, depression, loneliness, and anxiety.* We cannot give up on each other. We cannot give up on ourselves.

In our body, there are neurological and biological pathways that are influenced by our interactions. These interactions can happen as part of the nervous system, immune system, and endocrine (hormone) system.[4,8] Cortisol (the stress hormone) and oxytocin (the love hormone) are just a couple examples of hormones that are moved by our social connections. There are also behavioral influences from our interactions. For example, our social circle can impact our eating, drinking, and exercise habits. Behavioral influences can lead to good and even bad habits. For example, excessive drinking or smoking.

Pick your social circles carefully and have enough confidence to not give in to peer pressure.

In the heart lays one of the most fascinating and saddest proofs of how our emotional associations impact our physical health. The broken heart syndrome. John Hopkins Medicine describes broken heart syndrome as "stress cardiomyopathy" where the heart muscle is weakened after sudden exposure to acute stress.[9] We hear about cases of broken heart syndrome when people are grieving for their loved ones.

Our surroundings (see Chapter Three), whether physical or social, play a large role in our wellbeing. Keep that in mind and take action to surround yourself with what is good for you. As Nobel Prize winners Daniel Kahneman, PhD and Angus Deaton, PhD showed, loneliness prevents us from experiencing positive emotions such as happiness and enjoyment. Loneliness indicated higher incidences of worry, stress, and sadness.[10] Kahneman and Deaton studied if money can buy happiness. Even though money improves the quality of life and one's thoughts on their life (life evaluation), at a certain level of income, money does not buy happiness. Happiness was described as the emotional wellbeing in experiencing joy, fascination, anxiety, sadness, anger, and affection.[10] It is hard to experience happiness alone. *Happiness, like most emotions in social beings, is meant to be shared.*

The National Academies of Sciences, Engineering, and Medicine highlighted statistics on how lonely and isolated older adults are.[11] The 2020 report states that,

> "Approximately one-quarter of community-dwelling Americans aged 65 and older are considered to be socially isolated, and a significant proportion of adults in the United States report feeling lonely. People who are 50 years of age or older are more likely to experience many of the risk factors that can cause or exacerbate social isolation or loneliness, such as living alone, the loss of family or friends, chronic illness, and sensory impairments." *The National Academies of Sciences, Engineering, and Medicine, 2020*[11]

These statistics are not just for the elderly. Vulnerable populations, underserved communities, low income individuals and families, children, and genders experience loneliness in various ways. To make it worse, the pandemic exasperated these numbers. A Harvard 2021 report reminds us of the high cost of loneliness in terms of physical, emotional, and substance/domestic abuse problems. The report also draws attention to young adults' loneliness as they are more likely to now suffer anxiety and depression.[12] The Harvard study shows that,

"Alarming numbers of Americans are lonely. According to our recent national survey of approximately 950 Americans, 36% of respondents reported feeling lonely "frequently" or "almost all the time or all the time" in the prior four weeks. A startling 61% of young people aged 18-25 and 51% of mothers with young children reported these miserable degrees of loneliness. Survey respondents also reported substantial increases in loneliness since the outbreak of the pandemic." *Harvard Making Caring Common Project, 2021*[12]

The hardest part of the Harvard report for me to

read was that: about half of the lonely young adults reported that no one, in the last few weeks, genuinely cared to take more than a few minutes to ask how they were doing. So make it a point, young and old, to ask your people how they are doing. Not casually but "really how are things going these days? How are you feeling? Where are you spending the majority of your time? Are you happy with your school/work/house etc.?" Make it a point to listen and care. If needed, a hug goes a long way. Even a virtual hug.[13]

The pandemic made many of us temporary germaphobes. I know I still worry more than I need to about germs, viruses, and anyone who coughs around me. If your temporary germophobia becomes chronic and starts interfering with your life, seek professional help. Known as Illness Anxiety Disorder (IAD), this chronic fear can be disruptive and reduce your quality of life. Know that it was probably triggered by a life event and that cognitive therapy can help you. Yet, it is imperative to recognize that interpersonal touch is important for regulating emotions.

There are endless studies on the physiological effects of touch and hugs from early childhood on. Recognize situational awareness, cultural differences, and appropriateness before you decide to give someone a hug. Sometimes a tap on the shoulder is genuinely comforting. *I usually cross both my hands onto my own shoulders and say, "giving you a hug."* If the person wants this hug, they usually lean in and hug you. If not, it is enough to let them know they are cared for. It is comforting to them to know that you do care.

Last but not least, the Harvard report brings up an important recommendation. This one depends on only yourself. The recommendation is to manage self-defeating thoughts and behaviors that can also fuel loneliness.[12] For more on confidence and establishing a brand for yourself, read Chapter Four of this book. So go ahead, have the confidence to share yourself with the world around you in a meaningful way.

SOCIALIZATION AT WORK

A balanced life/work approach and personal/professional separation are important in preventing burnout. Yet, socialization in the form of interacting and engaging at work is also imperative. New research conducted in Vietnam surveyed 675 recently employed graduates (< five years of work experience; < 35 years old).[14] *Survey results show that socialization tactics can promote proactive behavior and engagement at work.* This is known as "organizational socialization tactics" and the end result expected is better work engagement between both the organization and the individual.

With the new remote and hybrid working tools and schedules made available to us during the COVID-19 pandemic, more employees and employers are comfortable and productive working remotely from home. Just because we are remote, it should not mean that we are isolated. I prefer the hybrid model. Hybrid schedules reduce video conferencing and allow remote work while presenting more opportunities for dynamic face-to-face interactions. To me, this is the best of both worlds that allow us to focus and be productive at home with less commute time. Depending on the field, this hybrid working model allows more in-person brainstorming and successful project delivery. Interaction is not only important among staff members but also important with the company as a living and growing unit.

Companies are more than office buildings. Company cultures should grow and adapt by igniting employee development. Give your staff a multitude of reasons to stay loyal and grow with you. In recent years we have witnessed higher than usual turnover in the workplace. A successful company is a company that will encourage proactive employees that will grow within and for the company. A successful company does not undervalue the physical health, mental wellbeing, and time management of its employees.

Part of valuing the employee's wellbeing is creating avenues for the workers to interact and express their opinions. Organizations can provide avenues for better staff interaction through offering programs like:

- After-work activities (example: bowling or pickleball leagues, book clubs, guest speaker events, classes, and volunteering after hours).
- Milestone achievement celebrations.
- Monthly or quarterly breakfast, potluck, or cake for birthdays or work anniversaries.
- Company picnics.

There are many events companies can plan to interact with their employees and thank them for their contributions. However, honest, direct, and proper communication remains equally critical. *Surveying employees (and doing something about the results) is very telling about the company culture.*

First impressions are also significant. Employers should be well prepared during onboarding to actively engage incoming staff in the company culture. Handing a new employee a laptop and sending them back home remotely or to their desk is not optimal.

Create events to attract new workers into your culture so they want to become part of it.

The same responsibility falls on the employee. Even if your company does not provide the best avenues for professional socialization, you can always schedule a working lunch or a lunch-walk with a colleague. Make your presence known. Let upper management also notice you by dressing and conveying yourself in a professional and proactive manner, even when working remotely. Drop by using an email, or schedule a virtual call or meeting to keep in touch.

I always appreciate it when I get an email or a message that reads, "I am reaching out to check in. We have not connected for a while. Hope all is well with you. Would you have availability next week to catch up?" I find these requests caring and engaging. Whether these requests come from friends or colleagues, I appreciate them. Especially given our busy schedules. It is nice being thought of, no matter where you work and how busy or important you are.

⊘ TRY THIS: FIND YOUR VILLAGE!

Try Different Places to Interact: You do not have to be an extrovert, but you need your village. These are only a few suggestions to ignite some ideas within you. Make an effort to socialize and connect a little more. These connections should feel safe and fun. *Privacy and time to reflect on your own are still very important.* So do not go extreme and unbalance your routine. Try to form social connections in your community. Try:

- Recreational sports, running groups, and local leagues.
- A gym, yoga studio, or other fitness centers.
- Book clubs.
- Creative groups such as knitting, quilting, art, painting, wood carving, carpentry, beer making, mixology, and author workshops.
- Gardening communities or volunteer at botanical centers.
- A place of worship.

- Neighborhood events.

- Volunteering at food banks and charity events.

- Traveling by different means: bus, subway, ship, train, boat, or plane. Enjoy the journey.

- Creating your own hobby-driven community activities and groups. Share your hobbies and talents.

- Tapping into municipal parks and recreational activities. This includes local library events, senior/youth centers, and community education events.

Make the First Move: Many times I have witnessed children ask each other, "do you want to be friends?" The many times children run to their parents in a playground and say "I made a new friend, please exchange numbers" so the kids can see each other again. It is so cute and lovable. As adults, it may not be as cute running up to someone and asking, "Can we be friends?" However, we can show interest by planning activities with people we meet that may have something in common with us. These activities can lead to friendships. For example, you learn that someone you work with enjoys playing racquetball. It is also a hobby of yours. Make the first move and say, "I usually play at this gym next door on Saturday mornings. Would you like to play a match?"

Your coworker might love to play a match or might have a legit excuse to set up a different day and time. The person might even flat out not be interested, and that is also okay. You tried. You stepped out of your comfort zone and you asked. Make an effort to build a community around you. Do not be afraid of rejection. We all have been rejected multiple times in our lives. This racquetball friend might turn into a best friend or just an acquaintance you get some good workouts with every now and then. There are no expectations except making sure that you continue meeting different people and engaging with your community.

Another example, invite neighbors to create a book club. There is a book you really would like to read. This book will even be made into a movie in theatres soon. Use your community HOA listing or strike a conversation with neighbors about the book. If the conversation flows, gather up additional friends and neighbors, and create a book club and movie events to go with it.

Sometimes it is difficult to know where to start finding friends or creating a social network. It is harder for adults to make friends. Even finding acquaintances to plan activities and go to events with is not easy. Everyone's schedule is packed. We are all exhausted or overworked. Sometimes we do not even want to make friends. We are perfectly comfortable in our little circle or alone at home. Which is the objective of this chapter, *do not get used to being alone and isolated.*

So how do you make friends? Can you make friends outside of meeting people at school, work, church, favorite coffee shop, or in your neighborhood? Start with proximity - whoever is sitting or standing next to you.[15] New research outlines that students sitting next to each other are more likely to form friendships. Even when seating arrangements changed, new friendships were formed.[15] This research is based on elementary aged children. Sometimes simply learning from kids' innocent behavior is the best approach. So next time you are in line waiting, sitting at a doctor's office, look around you and say hi to someone next to you. Strike a conversation. Give a compliment. The friendship may or may not form.

Being social requires interacting and learning from others. Those interactions do not all need to become deeply bonded friendships.

Just be kind to people and be brave enough to compliment them. You might just make their day if nothing else. Be extra kind to the elderly. Sometimes I feel that as a society we forget about them. If you ever strike up a conversation with an elderly, they will usually welcome it and engage you through it. They have many stories to tell and lessons learned in life. I learned my lesson one day while rushing down the tea aisle in a grocery store. A beautiful elderly woman paused in the same aisle and asked me if I was in a

CHAPTER FIVE

rush. It took me by surprise.

Was I in a rush?

Do I look like I am in a rush?

Was I rude passing her by?

I thought to myself, "who am I kidding? I am always in a rush for one reason or another." I slowed down a bit and looked apologetically at her. The elderly woman continued saying, "I have no rush to go anywhere these days. If I do, it is like rushing to the grave."

That statement stays with me now in every aisle and every situation. Does that mean I slowed down? Unfortunately, I still need to hustle, but I do so with more purpose these days. I still find myself part of a busy schedule, short days, places to be, and rushing to go. However, I did slow down. I especially slow down in the grocery aisles and when I see an elderly person I pause. I even try to make conversation instead of passing people by. Sometimes, if I see someone pondering a product in the market, I ask them if they like it. I even show them my favorite brand. It really is such a different perspective and experience than playing race carts in the supermarket.

Now, just to be completely honest, the introvert in me still prefers to shop in quiet times. But I try harder to interact positively and socially when the opportunity presents itself. I even make it a point to compliment something I like about someone. Their pretty eyes, cool clay earrings, the book they are reading, their haircut, the color of their nail polish or shirt. It makes people smile - and it brings me happiness. I said applying this chapter is hard. It is even harder for me. I am trying my best to practice what I preach.

Many adults with children engage through their kids' activities and sports leagues. When the kids grow up and move to college or start driving by themselves, the empty nest syndrome might set in. This is the best time for adults to venture out, try different activities, and meet new people in their community. It is okay to grow out of certain events, and people, as long as you continue participating in different activities. You will make a few friends throughout the years that are worth millions. Great friendships are hard to come across. Make sure you cherish the ones you have by verbalizing that no matter what is going on in your life, your close friends know that you care about them. Make that phone call, check in often, and be there when they need you.

Ask the Right Questions: When you meet people, ask them questions to help drive the conversation beyond the weather. Find something in common. Do not forget to compliment them. You will leave them with a smile. Ask about their hobbies or places they like to vacation. Ask about their favorite local restaurants. Somehow I find myself always trapped in conversations everyone tells you not to discuss with people: politics and religion, for example. Certain individuals are actually amazing to learn from, and I enjoy the dynamics of their thoughts. Just be respectful. If you do not agree, this is not the time to prove your point. This is the time to socialize and connect and understand different viewpoints. This is not the time to lecture and get angry if someone does not agree with you. Find topics you can dialogue on passionately and respectfully. Casually walk away from conversations that are not conducive to a respectful and positive exchange.

Last But Not Least, Recharge: Being social does not mean getting overwhelmed by people or schedules. Always leave time for you to recharge and spend time away from routine and chaos. Plan a vacation or staycation. Use this paid time off that many Americans accumulate and do not use. Spend time alone or take a break from social media. Check your cellphone usage. You will be surprised how many hours a day we use our cellphones. Set a goal to use your cellphone less for a few days. Take walks, watch non-stressful shows on TV, and read books. Go to a bookstore and walk around. Give yourself time to recharge.

In general, say "yes" to more opportunities in your life. It takes courage to say "yes" more and you grow through it. In the meantime, it takes even more courage to stay firm on your "no" when you know an interaction is not for you or you need a mental break. Balance your life and your schedule. Stay social, and engage with your community and yourself in a meaningful way. Remember, not everyone can be your best friend, but there is value in social interactions for self-growth and development.

CONCLUSION
The Equanimous

Equanimous, your mind is calm, and your thoughts are composed. Be at ease, take a breath. Remain true to yourself because you know what an amazing person you are and how hard you work. This polished draft of you will dust you off from the last few years that have roughed you up. You are now better prepared to thrive in an ever-changing society.

Keep in mind that the key to success is consistency over time. Whether in financial investments and compounding interest, diet and exercise, or learning new skills and languages, consistency is crucial.

Consistency is a long-term process. When you fail, try again. Do not give up. Repeat the positive actions that help you reach your goals. Be constructive in setting your goals to pursue your success and happiness. For example, I may never be an Olympic swimmer, no matter how hard I try. However, I can become more fit and organized in my day if I dedicate myself to a disciplined early morning swim routine.

Take a moment now that you have read this book, set your goals, and really ✅ **TRY THIS**. Try this for your self-development. Do not be concerned with what others may think. Your true support system will shine through during this process. Grant yourself this peace and grace we started out with in Chapter One. Learn to use your time wisely like we learned in Chapter Two. Surround yourself with things that heal you like we designed in Chapter Three. Visualize the charismatic, confident, and collected person reconstructed by the end of Chapter Four. Finally, share yourself with the world and lead your village as outlined in Chapter Five. Start this new edition, *The Second Draft* of you with a celebration.

Celebrate by spreading joy through a good deed. Pay for someone's groceries or food in the drive through lane. Hand a gift card to the elderly gentleman mowing the grass off the road on a hot day, and let them enjoy a cold beverage on you. Bake a cake for a neighbor or colleague who is having a rough time this week. Let your spouse or parent sleep in and take over their chores today. Any random act of kindness will do.

Continue the celebration and break away from your routine today. No need to plan a big event. Insert things in your schedule that make you happy with purpose. Sometimes all it takes is a cup of coffee or tea. Take five minutes sipping it alone outside or in a cozy corner. Do not forget to turn on the "coffeehouse/jazz/chill" music station in the background. You can find these stations on music apps on your cellphone or on the radio. Do keep that phone on DND. Create this simple moment and exist in it.

We strive to be organized, organized houses, organized schedules, and organized sports. We learned how to plan to be productive and efficient. Now and then, we will take a break to reward ourselves by doing something out of the ordinary. Something as simple as going to a new restaurant in a different part of town can feel like a mini travel vacation. Breakfast omelets for dinner? How about gathering your family or randomly calling a friend to go on a quick road trip to a state park? If you have teenagers at home, I can already see them rolling their eyes at this idea. Especially if you wake them up early in the morning. That is okay, every now and then you will remind your teenager (or grouchy friend) to look up from their cellphones and enjoy the journey along the way. You are making memories. One day they will look back and appreciate it. Take a photo and treasure the moment.

Whatever you choose to commemorate this new edit of yourself, just remember:

> "The fruit of the spirit is love, joy, peace, forbearance, kindness, goodness, faithfulness, gentleness and self-control. Against such things there is no law." *Galatians[1]*

So you do you, *The Second Draft* of you. Be confident and convinced because you know that you are guided by all things good and graceful.

All the good wishes,
Mia

CHAPTER ONE: The Fortune Teller

The power of being understood:

- ○ Acknowledge Your Own Resilience
- ○ Verbally Ask For and Offer Help
- ○ Mimicking and Mirroring
- ○ Regulate Your Response During Conflict
- ○ Never Look Back at Toxic People
- ○ Notes & Ideas

_____
_____
_____
_____
_____
_____
_____
_____
_____
_____
_____
_____
_____
_____
_____
_____
_____
_____
_____
_____

CHAPTER TWO: The More Time I Have

Start your day with a clear strategy to improve your productivity:

○ Protect Your Time
○ Plan Your Day
○ Influence Your Willpower
○ Avoid Procrastination
○ Organize and Conquer
○ Check Out the Pomodoro Technique
○ Set Your State of Mind
○ Notes & Ideas

_____
_____
_____
_____
_____
_____
_____
_____
_____
_____
_____
_____
_____
_____
_____
_____
_____
_____
_____

CHAPTER THREE: If These Walls Could Talk

Our physical space impacts our mental one:

- ○ Safety First
- ○ Music
- ○ Brighter Rooms, Brighter You (Phototherapy/Light Therapy)
- ○ Biophilic Design
- ○ Art and Expression (Aesthetic Therapy)
- ○ Furnishing, Signaling and Wayfinding
- ○ Notes & Ideas

_____
_____
_____
_____
_____
_____
_____
_____
_____
_____
_____
_____
_____
_____
_____
_____
_____
_____
_____
_____
_____
_____

CHAPTER FOUR: I Wish I Were Special

You are, show it:

○ Go to that Annual Check Up

○ Exercise Your Confidence

○ New Me, New Look

○ Simplify, Simplify, Simplify

○ You Are Your Toughest Critic

○ Lift Your Head Up, Literally and Figuratively

○ Practice that Elevator Speech

○ Vocabulary and Voice Tone

○ Beware Imposter Syndrome

○ Notes & Ideas

_____

_____

_____

_____

_____

_____

_____

_____

_____

_____

_____

_____

_____

_____

_____

_____

_____

CHAPTER FIVE: The Life of the Party

You do not have to be an extrovert, but you need your village:

○ Try Different Places to Interact
○ Make the First Move
○ Ask the Right Questions
○ Last But Not Least, Recharge
○ Notes & Ideas

_____
_____
_____
_____
_____
_____
_____
_____
_____
_____
_____
_____
_____
_____
_____
_____
_____
_____
_____
_____
_____
_____

NOTES

Introduction

1-Forbes (2021). Empathy is the Most Important Leadership Skill. by Tracy Brower. September 19, 2021.

2-Qualtrics (2020). Confronting mental health crisis stemming from the COVID-19 pandemic. Qualtrics. April 14, 2020. Retrieved June 10, 2022, from https://www.qualtrics.com/blog/confronting-mental-health/.

3-APA Dictionary of Psychology. (n.d.). https://dictionary.apa.org/.

4-Think with Krys Boyd (2022). Here's why you're burned out at work. Interview with Jonathan Malesic. May 18, 2022. Originally aired on January 25, 2022. KERA North Texas. https://think.kera.org/2022/05/18/heres-why-youre-burned-out-at-work/.

5-Kashyap, E., & Kaur, S. (2021). Importance of Work Life Balance: A Review. Elementary Education Online, 20(5), 5068-5068.

6-Grigg, N.S. (2006). Workforce development and knowledge management in water utilities. Journal - American Water Works Association, 98: 91-99. https://doi.org/10.1002/j.1551-8833.2006.tb07756.x.

7-Frigo, M. (2006). Knowledge retention: A guide for utilities. Journal - American Water Works Association, 98: 81-84. https://doi.org/10.1002/j.1551-8833.2006.tb07754.x.

8-ASCE Forum (2021). Water and Wastewater Systems and Utilities: Challenges and Opportunities during the COVID-19 Pandemic. J. Water Resour. Plann. Manage., 147(5): 02521001.

9-Robb, D. (2005). Draining the talent pool: many utilities face the loss of 50 percent or more of their technical workforce in the next ten years. What can be done to head off this looming crisis in technical and engineering talent?. Power Engineering, 109(5), 46-49.

10-Orr, J., & Deitz, R. (2006). A leaner, more skilled US manufacturing workforce. Current Issues in Economics and Finance, 12(2).

11-Trump, D. J. (2017). Presidential executive order

on assessing and strengthening the manufacturing and defense industrial base and supply chain resiliency of the United States.

Chapter One
1-Merriam Webster Dictionary (1928). Online at https://www.merriam-webster.com/dictionary/emotion.

2-Catalyst (2021). Empathy Is a Force for Innovation, Flourishing, and Intent to Stay. https://www.catalyst.org/reports/empathy-work-strategy-crisis.

3-Pérez-Manrique, A., & Gomila, A. (2022). Emotional contagion in nonhuman animals: A review. Wiley Interdisciplinary Reviews: Cognitive Science, 13(1), e1560

4-Grant, E. T. (2021). 11 weird habits you didn't know dogs adopt from their owners. Bustle. December 20, 2021. Retrieved June 21, 2022, from https://www.bustle.com/life/dog-habits-that-mimic-owners.

5-Gallup, A. C. (2021). On the link between emotional contagion and contagious yawning.

Neuroscience & Biobehavioral Reviews, 121, 18-19.

6-Lee, M. T., & Theokary, C. (2021). The superstar social media influencer: Exploiting linguistic style and emotional contagion over content?. Journal of Business Research, 132, 860-871.

7-Aron, E. N. (2013). The highly sensitive person: How to thrive when the world overwhelms you. Kensington Publishing Corp..

8-Greven, C. U., Lionetti, F., Booth, C., Aron, E. N., Fox, E., Schendan, H. E., ... & Homberg, J. (2019). Sensory processing sensitivity in the context of environmental sensitivity: A critical review and development of research agenda. Neuroscience & Biobehavioral Reviews, 98, 287-305.

9-Southwick, S. M., Sippel, L., Krystal, J., Charney, D., Mayes, L., & Pietrzak, R. (2016). Why are some individuals more resilient than others: the role of social support. World psychiatry: official journal of the World Psychiatric Association (WPA), 15(1), 77–79. https://doi.org/10.1002/wps.20282.

10-Shear, M. K. (2022). Grief and mourning gone awry: pathway and course of complicated grief.

Dialogues in clinical neuroscience.

11-Wetherell, J. L. (2012). Complicated grief therapy as a new treatment approach, Dialogues in Clinical Neuroscience, 14:2, 159-166, DOI: 10.31887/DCNS.2012.14.2/jwetherell.

12-Marshall, B. J. (2009). Silent grief: Narratives of bereaved adult siblings. University of Toronto.

13-Lunansky, G., van Borkulo, C., Blanken, T., Cramer, A. O. J., & Borsboom, D. (2022). Bouncing back from life's perturbations: Formalizing psychological resilience from a complex systems perspective. February 28, 2022. https://doi.org/10.31234/osf.io/ftx4j.

14-Deshmukh, M., & Mutreja, C. D. L. (2022). Measuring the Effectiveness of Intervention Program on Adversity Quotient of the college students. International Journal of Early Childhood, 14(03), 2022.

15-Stoltz, P. (1997). Adversity quotient: Turning obstacles into opportunities. New York: Wiley, ISBN 978-0471344131.

16-PEAK Learning, (n.d.).
https://www.peaklearning.com.

17-Gschwandtner, G. (2020). How to Manage Adversity during a crisis by Dr. Paul Stoltz. Interview with Dr. Paul Stoltz. Selling Power. May 19, 2020 https://www.youtube.com/watch?v=HBUY5KLvfVI &list=RDLVWfHzjkLtQGM&index=3.

18-Stoltz, P. (2020). AQ, the core of our inheritance. TED^{x}HotelschoolTheHague. March 31, 2020. https://www.youtube.com/watch?v=BOqeIOCcC9M &list=RDLVWfHzjkLtQGM&index=2.

19-American Psychological Association topics on Emotional Health. (n.d.). https://www.apa.org/topics.

20-The Bible. New International Version (NIV James 1:19)
https://www.bible.com/search/bible?query=james%2 01:19.

Chapter Two
1-Cambridge Dictionary
https://dictionary.cambridge.org/dictionary/english/p roductivity.

2-Brumby, D. P., Janssen, C. P., & Mark, G. (2019). How do interruptions affect productivity?. In Rethinking productivity in software engineering (pp. 85-107). A press, Berkeley, CA.

3-Mark, G., Iqbal, S., Czerwinski, M., & Johns, P. (2015, February). Focused, aroused, but so distractible: Temporal perspectives on multitasking and communications. In Proceedings of the 18th ACM Conference on Computer Supported Cooperative Work & Social Computing (pp. 903-916).

4-Rosekind, M. R., Gregory, K. B., Mallis, M. M., Brandt, S. L., Seal, B., & Lerner, D. (2010). The cost of poor sleep: workplace productivity loss and associated costs. Journal of Occupational and Environmental Medicine, 91-98.

5-Rastogi, A., Pati, S. P., Krishnan, T. N., & Krishnan, S. (2018). Causes, contingencies, and consequences of disengagement at work: An integrative literature review. Human Resource Development Review, 17(1), 62-94.

6-Markos, S., & Sridevi, M. S. (2010). Employee

engagement: The key to improving performance. International journal of business and management, 5(12), 89.

7-Hasan, H., Nikmah, F., Nurbaya, S., Fiernaningsih, N., & Wahyu, E. (2021). A review of employee engagement: Empirical studies. Management Science Letters, 11(7), 1969-1978.

8-Albrecht, S. L., Green, C. R., & Marty, A. (2021). Meaningful work, job resources, and employee engagement. Sustainability, 13(7), 4045.

9-Steinhorst, C. (2020, February 28). How To Reclaim The Huge Losses That Multitasking Forces On Your Company. Forbes.

10-PWC. Special Report: Financial stress and the bottom line. PWC. https://www.pwc.com/us/en/private-company-services/publications/assets/pwc-financial-stress-and-bottom-line.pdf.

11-Halkos, G., & Bousinakis, D. (2010). The effect of stress and satisfaction on productivity. International Journal of Productivity and Performance Management.

12-Liza, V. (2011). Stress management techniques: Evidence-based procedures that reduce stress and promote health. Health science journal, 5(2), 0-0.

13-Frew, D. R. (1974). Transcendental Meditation and productivity. Academy of Management Journal, 17(2), 362-368.

14-Nickerson, C. (2021). The Yerkes-Dodson Law and Performance. Simply Psychology.

15-Loh, K. K., & Kanai, R. (2014). Higher media multi-tasking activity is associated with smaller gray-matter density in the anterior cingulate cortex. Plos one, 9(9), e106698.

16-Brown, E. G. (2014). The time bandit solution: Recovering stolen time you never knew you had. Greenleaf Book Group.

17-Aeon, B., & Aguinis, H. (2017). It's about time: New perspectives and insights on time management. Academy of management perspectives, 31(4), 309-330.

18-Aeon, B., Faber, A., & Panaccio, A. (2021). Does

time management work? A meta-analysis. PloS one, 16(1), e0245066.

19-Michie, S. (2002). Causes and management of stress at work. Occupational and environmental medicine, 59(1), 67-72.

20-Kühnel, J., Zacher, H., De Bloom, J., & Bledow, R. (2017). Take a break! Benefits of sleep and short breaks for daily work engagement. European Journal of Work and Organizational Psychology, 26(4), 481-491.

21-Kelly, S. (2018, June 6). It's about time: Immediate rewards boost motivation. Cornell Chronicle.

22-Lunenburg, F. C. (2011). Goal-setting theory of motivation. International journal of management, business, and administration, 15(1), 1-6.

23-Zainal, H. (2017, September). Influence of work motivation and discipline on work productivity. In 2nd International Conference on Education, Science, and Technology (ICEST 2017) (pp. 25-27). Atlantis Press.

24-Duckworth, A. L., & Seligman, M. E. (2005). Self-discipline outdoes IQ in predicting academic performance of adolescents. Psychological science, 16(12), 939-944.

25-Ryan, N. (2012). Willpower: Rediscovering the greatest human strength, by Roy F. Baumeister and John Tierney.

26-Evans, P., & McPherson, G. E. (2015). Identity and practice: The motivational benefits of a long-term musical identity. Psychology of Music, 43(3), 407-422.

27-Tice, D. M., & Baumeister, R. F. (1997). Longitudinal study of procrastination, performance, stress, and health: The costs and benefits of dawdling. Psychological science, 8(6), 454-458.

28-Zacharia, J. (2015, September 24). The Bing "Marshmallow Studies": 50 Years of Continuing Research. Stanford Bing Nursery School.

29-Tracy, B. (2017). Eat that frog! 21 great ways to stop procrastinating and get more done in less time. Berrett-Koehler Publishers.

30-Habbert, R., & Schroeder, J. (2020). To build efficacy, eat the frog first: People misunderstand how the difficulty-ordering of tasks influences efficacy. Journal of Experimental Social Psychology, 91, 104032.

31-Amabile, T. M., & Kramer, S. J. (2011). The power of small wins. Harvard business review, 89(5), 70-80.

32-Microsoft Corporation. (2021). The next great disruption is hybrid work: are we ready?.

33-Laker, B., Pereira, V., Budhwar, P., & Malik, A. (2022). The surprising impact of meeting-free days. MIT Sloan Management Review.

34-Cirillo, F. (2018). The Pomodoro technique: The life-changing time-management system. Random House.

35-American Friends of Tel Aviv University. (2011, November 2). Finding relief in ritual: A healthy dose of repetitive behavior reduces anxiety, says researcher. ScienceDaily.

36-Resnick, M. L., & Zanotti, A. (1997). Using

ergonomics to target productivity improvements. Computers & Industrial Engineering, 33(1-2), 185-188.

37-Straker, L. M., Pollock, C. M., & Mangharam, J. E. (1997). The effect of shoulder posture on performance, discomfort and muscle fatigue whilst working on a visual display unit. International Journal of Industrial Ergonomics, 20(1), 1-10.

38-Gordon, J. (2012). The positive dog: A story about the power of positivity. John Wiley & Sons.

39-Malinsky, G. (2021). Harvard professor: Outsourcing chores could make you as happy as getting an $18,000 raise. CNBC Health and Wellness. Published Jan 23 2021 10:30 AM EST. Updated Thu, Jul 21 2022 8:40 AM EDT.

Chapter Three
1-Karakas, T., & Yildiz, D. (2020). Exploring the influence of the built environment on human experience through a neuroscience approach: A systematic review. Frontiers of Architectural Research, 9(1), 236–247. https://doi.org/10.1016/j.foar.2019.10.005.

2-Elnakat, A., D. Gomez, J., & Wright, M. (2016). A measure to manage approach to characterizing the energy impact of residential building stocks. AIMS Energy, 4(4), 574–588.
https://doi.org/10.3934/energy.2016.4.574.

3-Joon-Ho, C., Schiler, M., Xiaoxin, L. Bernadette, W., & Ferguson, K. (2018). Final Report: Human-Building Integration: Occupant Eye Pupil Size-Driven Lighting Control As a Sustainable Indoor Environmental Control Strategy in a Built Environment. US EPA Grant Number SU839276.

4-Vert, C.et al. (2020). Physical and mental health effects of repeated short walks in a blue space environment: A randomized crossover study. Environmental Research, 188, 109812–.
https://doi.org/10.1016/j.envres.2020.109812.

5-Oxford Reference
https://www.oxfordreference.com/.

6-Scannell, L., & Gifford, R. (2010). Defining place attachment: A tripartite organizing framework. Journal of Environmental Psychology, 30(1), 1–10.
https://doi.org/10.1016/j.jenvp.2009.09.006.

7-Stedman, R. (2003). Is It Really Just a Social Construction?: The Contribution of the Physical Environment to Sense of Place. Society & Natural Resources, 16(8), 671–685. https://doi.org/10.1080/08941920309189.

8-Gifford, R. (2014). Environmental Psychology Matters. Annual Review of Psychology, 65(1), 541–579. https://doi.org/10.1146/annurev-psych-010213-115048.

9-Ulrich RS. (1984). View through a Window May Influence Recovery from Surgery. Science (American Association for the Advancement of Science), 224(4647), 420–421. https://doi.org/10.1126/science.6143402.

10-Kweon, B., Ulrich, R., Walker, V., & Tassinary, L. (2008). Anger and Stress: The Role of Landscape Posters in an Office Setting. Environment and Behavior, 40(3), 355–381. https://doi.org/10.1177/0013916506298797.

11-Raanaas RK, Evensen KH, Rich D, Sjostrom G, Patil C. (2011). Benefits of indoor plants on attention capacity in an office setting. Journal of Environmental

Psychology. 31:99–105.

12-Connellan, K., Gaardboe, M., Riggs, D., Due, C., Reinschmidt, A., & Mustillo, L. (2013). Stressed Spaces: Mental Health and Architecture. HERD Journal, 6(4), 127–168. https://doi.org/10.1177/193758671300600408.

13-Beauchemin, K. M. & Hays, P. (1996). Sunny hospital rooms expedite recovery from severe and refractory depressions. Journal of Affective Disorders, 40(1), 49–51. doi:10.1016/0165-0327(96)00040-7.

14-Lorenz, S. G. (2007). The potential of the patient room to promote healing and well-being in patients and nurses. Holistic Nursing Practice, 21(5), 263–277.

15-Andes, M., & Shattell, M. M. (2006). An exploration of the meanings of space and place in acute psychiatric care. Issues in Mental Health Nursing, 27(6), 699–707. doi:10.1080/01612840600643057.

16-Daykin, N., Byrne E., Soteriou, T., & O'Connor, S. (2008). The impact of art, design and environment in mental health care: A systematic review of the literature. Journal of the Royal Society for the Promotion of Health, 128(2), 85–94.

17-Mallawaarachchi, H., De Silva, L., & Rameezdeen, R. (2017). Modelling the relationship between green built environment and occupants' productivity. Facilities (Bradford, West Yorkshire, England), 35(3/4), 170–187. https://doi.org/10.1108/F-07-2015-0052.

18-Lee, H., & Park, S. (2018). Assessment of Importance and Characteristics of Biophilic Design Patterns in a Children's Library. Sustainability (Basel, Switzerland), 10(4), 987. https://doi.org/10.3390/su10040987.

19-Xue, F., Gou, Z., Lau, S., Lau, S., Chung, K., & Zhang, J. (2019). From biophilic design to biophilic urbanism: Stakeholders' perspectives. Journal of Cleaner Production, 211, 1444–1452. https://doi.org/10.1016/j.jclepro.2018.11.277.

20-Beatley, T. (2016). Handbook of Biophilic City Planning and Design. Island Press, Washington, DC.

21-A Prescription for Nature (2020). PaRx Program.

BC Parks Foundation, Canada.
https://www.parkprescriptions.ca/en/about.

22-Joy James, J., Christiana, R.W., & Battista, R.A. (2019). A historical and critical analysis of park prescriptions, Journal of Leisure Research, 50:4, 311-329, DOI: 10.1080/00222216.2019.1617647.

Chapter Four

1-Mahon, J. F., & Wartick, S. L. (2003). Dealing with stakeholders: How reputation, credibility and framing influence the game. Corporate reputation review, 6(1), 19-35.

2-Számadó, S., Balliet, D., Giardini, F., Power, E. A., & Takács, K. (2021). The language of cooperation: reputation and honest signalling. Philosophical Transactions of the Royal Society B, 376(1838), 20200286.

3-Orth, U. (2018). The family environment in early childhood has a long-term effect on self-esteem: A longitudinal study from birth to age 27 years. Journal of Personality and Social Psychology, 114(4), 637–655. https://doi.org/10.1037/pspp0000143.

4-Orth, U., & Robins, R. W. (2014). The Development of Self-Esteem. Current Directions in Psychological Science, 23(5), 381–387. https://doi.org/10.1177/0963721414547414.

5-Rath, T. (2007). Strengths Finder 2.0. New York: Gallup Press.

6-Clifton Strengths Assessment by Gallup (2022). https://www.gallup.com/cliftonstrengths/en/253868/popular-cliftonstrengths-assessment-products.aspx.

7-Gates L, Lineberger MR, Crockett J, Hubbard J. (1988). Birth order and its relationship to depression, anxiety, and self-concept test scores in children. J Genet Psychol. 149:29–34. doi: 10.1080/00221325.1988.10532136.

8-Schwab MR, Lundgren DC. (1978). Birth order, perceived appraisals by significant others, and self-esteem. Psychol Rep. 43:443–54. doi: 10.2466/pr0.1978.43.2.443.

9-Kidwell JS. (1982). The neglected birth order: middleborns. J Marriage Fam. 44:225–35. doi: 10.2307/351276.

10-Fukuya, Y., Fujiwara, T., Isumi, A., Doi, S., & Ochi, M. (2021). Association of birth order with mental health problems, self-esteem, resilience, and happiness among children: Results from A-CHILD study. Frontiers in Psychiatry, 12. https://doi.org/10.3389/fpsyt.2021.638088.

11-Ben-Ze'ev, A. (2020). In the Name of Love: How Self-Esteem and Self-Confidence Power the Most Fulfilling Relationships. Psychology Today. December 22, 2020. https://www.psychologytoday.com/us/blog/in-the-name-love/202012/how-self-esteem-and-self-confidence-power-the-most-fulfilling.

12-Kay, K., & Shipman, C. (2014). The confidence gap. The Atlantic, 14(1), 1-18.

13-Psych2Go (2020). 4 Reasons Why You Feel Insecure About Yourself. April 5, 2020 https://psych2go.net/4-reasons-why-you-feel-insecure-about-yourself/.

14-Carver, C. S., & Scheier, M. F. (2019). Confidence, doubt, and coping with anxiety. In Anxiety: Recent developments in cognitive, psychophysiological, and health research (pp. 13-22).

Taylor & Francis.

15-Soysal, D., Bani-Yaghoub, M., & Riggers-Piehl, T. A. (2022). Analysis of anxiety, motivation, and confidence of STEM students during the COVID-19 pandemic. International Electronic Journal of Mathematics Education, 17(2), em0684.

16-Kang, H., & Jang, S. (2018). Effects of competition anxiety on self-confidence in soccer players: Modulation effects of home and away games. Journal of Men's Health, 14(3), 62-68.

17-Oviedo, V. Y., & Tree, J. E. F. (2021). Meeting by text or video-chat: Effects on confidence and performance. Computers in Human Behavior Reports, 3, 100054.

18-U.S. Centers for Disease Control and Prevention (2012). Second National Report on Biochemical Indicators of Diet and Nutrition in the U.S. Population. Atlanta, GA: National Center for Environmental Health; April 2012.

19-Cazzola, R., Della Porta, M., Manoni, M., Iotti, S., Pinotti, L., & Maier, J. A. (2020). Going to the roots of reduced magnesium dietary intake: A tradeoff

between climate changes and sources. Heliyon, 6(11), e05390.
https://doi.org/10.1016/j.heliyon.2020.e05390

20-Dweck CS (2006). Mindset: The new psychology of success. New York, NY: Random House

21-Cuddy, Amy (2012). TED Global 2012 - Your body language may shape who you are. https://www.ted.com/talks/amy_cuddy_your_body_l anguage_may_shape_who_you_are?language=en.

22-Kraus, M. W. (2017). Voice-only communication enhances empathic accuracy. American Psychologist, 72(7), 644–654.
https://doi.org/10.1037/amp0000147.

23-na (2020) How to Speak with Confidence and Sound Better.
https://www.scienceofpeople.com/speak-with-confidence/.

24-Puhl, R. M., & Himmelstein, M. S. (2018). A Word to the Wise: Adolescent Reactions to Parental Communication about Weight. Childhood obesity (Print), 14(5), 291–301.
https://doi.org/10.1089/chi.2018.0047.

25-Mandell B. F. (2018). The bias of word choice and the interpretation of laboratory tests. Cleveland Clinic journal of medicine, 85(8), 577–578. https://doi.org/10.3949/ccjm.85b.08018.

26-Irie, K., Zhao, S., Okamoto, K., & Liang, N. (2021). Examining the Effect of Adverbs and Onomatopoeia on Physical Movement. Frontiers in psychology, 4291.

27-Mainali S. (2020). Being an Imposter: Growing Out of Impostership. JNMA; journal of the Nepal Medical Association, 58(232), 1097–1099. https://doi.org/10.31729/jnma.5505.

28-Bravata, D. M., Watts, S. A., Keefer, A. L., Madhusudhan, D. K., Taylor, K. T., Clark, D. M., Nelson, R. S., Cokley, K. O., & Hagg, H. K. (2020). Prevalence, Predictors, and Treatment of Impostor Syndrome: a Systematic Review. Journal of general internal medicine, 35(4), 1252–1275. https://doi.org/10.1007/s11606-019-05364-1.

29-Palmer Chris. (2021). How to overcome impostor phenomenon. Monitor on Psychology. June 1, 2021, American Psychological Association Monitor on

Psychology Vol. 52 No. 4. Print version: Page 44
https://www.apa.org/monitor/2021/06/cover-
impostor-phenomenon.

30-Cabane, O. F. (2013). The charisma myth: How
anyone can master the art and science of personal
magnetism. Penguin.

31-Clark, Bryan. (2019). "What Makes People
Charismatic, and How You Can Be, Too." The New
York Times, The New York Times, 15 Aug. 2019.
https://www.nytimes.com/2019/08/15/smarter-
living/what-makes-people-charismatic-and-how-
you-can-be-too.html.

Chapter Five
1-Harlow, H. F. (1959). The development of learning
in the rhesus monkey. American Scientist.

2-Harlow, H. F., Dodsworth, R. O., & Harlow, M. K.
(1965). Total social isolation in monkeys.
Proceedings of the National Academy of Sciences,
54(1), 90-97.

3-Harlow, H. F., & Harlow, M. K. (1962). Social
Deprivation in Monkeys. Scientific American,
207(5), 136–150.

http://www.jstor.org/stable/24936357.

4-Weir, K. (2018). Life-saving relationships. Monitor on Psychology, 49(3). March 2018. https://www.apa.org/monitor/2018/03/life-saving-relationships.

5-Holt-Lunstad, J., Smith, T. B., & Layton, J. B. (2010). Social relationships and mortality risk: a meta-analytic review. PLoS medicine, 7(7), e1000316.

6-Hampton, K. N., Sessions, L. F., Her, E. J., & Rainie, L. (2009) Social isolation and new technology. Pew Internet & American Life Project, 4.

7-Whisman, M. A., Beach, S. R. H., & Snyder, D. K. (2008) Is marital discord taxonic and can taxonic status be assessed reliably? Results from a national, representative sample of married couples. Journal of Consulting and Clinical Psychology, 76(5), 745–755. https://doi.org/10.1037/0022-006X.76.5.745.

8-Uchino, B. N., & Way, B. M. (2017). Integrative pathways linking close family ties to health: A neurochemical perspective. American Psychologist, 72(6), 590–600.

https://doi.org/10.1037/amp0000049.

9-Wittstein, Ilan S. (n.d.). Broken Heart Syndrome. Health. Johns Hopkins Advanced Heart Failure Fellowship https://www.hopkinsmedicine.org/health/conditions-and-diseases/broken-heart-syndrome.

10-Kahneman, D., & Deaton, A. (2010). Does Money Buy Happiness. PNAS Early Edition.

11-National Academies of Sciences, Engineering, and Medicine. (2020). Social Isolation and Loneliness in Older Adults: Opportunities for the Health Care System. Washington, DC: The National Academies Press. https://doi.org/10.17226/25663.

12-Weissbourd, R., Batanova, M., Lovison, V., & Torres, E. (2021). Loneliness in America how the Pandemic Has Deepened an Epidemic of Loneliness and What We Can Do about it. Harvard Making Caring Common, 1-13.

13-Freeman, G., & Acena, D. (2021). Hugging from A Distance: Building Interpersonal Relationships in Social Virtual Reality. In ACM International Conference on Interactive Media Experiences June,

2021 (pp. 84-95).

14-Nguyen, T. N. T., Bui, T. H. T., & Nguyen, T. H. H. (2021). Improving employees' proactive behaviors at workplace: The role of organizational socialization tactics and work engagement. Journal of Human Behavior in the Social Environment, 31(6), 673-688.

15-Faur, S., & Laursen, B. (2022). Classroom Seat Proximity Predicts Friendship Formation. Frontiers in psychology, 2183.

Conclusion
1-The Bible. New International Version (NIV Galatians 5:22-23)
https://www.bible.com/bible/compare/GAL.5.22-23.

INDEX

action-sentence
  compatibility effect,
  120, 137
adversity, 15, 16, 17,
  18, 21, 26, 30, 32,
  185
Angus Deaton, PhD,
  149
anxiety, 2, 42, 92,
  100, 118, 119, 124,
  199, 200, 201
APA, 2, 138, 181
AQ, 16, 26, 27, 29,
  186
Art, 101
Ashley Whillans,
  PhD, 74
Biophilic, 94, 99, 197
Birth order, 112, 199
brand, 107, 108, 110,
  123, 127, 128
built environment, 8,
  79, 80, 81, 82, 83,
  84, 88, 89, 93, 96,
  99, 102, 193, 197
burnout, 2, 3, 18, 24
calories, 124
capsule wardrobe, 128
cellphone, 43, 44,
  166, 171

charisma, 107, 204
childhood, 111, 114,
  118, 135, 198
Childhood Obesity,
  136
cognitive behavioral
  therapy, 22
color, 1, 85, 92, 99
community, 88, 95,
  142, 143
compliment, 122, 162,
  164, 165
confidence, 107, 109,
  110, 112, 114, 115,
  116, 119, 120, 121,
  122, 123, 125, 126,
  131, 133, 135, 137,
  138, 139, 200, 201,
  202
  Amy Cuddy, PhD,
    131
  Carol Dweck, PhD,
    126
confident, 6, 8, 10, 11,
  34, 42, 115, 121,
  126, 128, 129, 134,
  135, 170, 173
conflict resolution,
  134
COVID-19, 2, 4, 85,

ABOUT THE AUTHOR
Mia Nakat, PhD

is a published author in peer-reviewed journals scoping the fields of environmental health sciences, sociodemographics, data analytics, resource conservation, and gender roles and influences. She has served as a court expert witness and is recognized by the House of Representatives 79th Texas Legislature for *"bridging the gap between scientific knowledge and its application to environmentally sound public policy..."*

Mia has over twenty years of experience, including twelve years of classroom and academic research. She lives in Texas with her husband, daughter, and two adopted fur babies.

GUEST AUTHOR
Chapter Two Contributor
Walid Ramady

is a Cornell engineering management graduate who worked over twenty years in engineering, construction, and risk management. He is involved in the successful execution of large scale industrial and data center projects.

Throughout his career, he utilized productivity tools and intricate schedules for effective project delivery and successful client services. Walid travels extensively. He is a citizen of the world and an outdoor enthusiast.

www.ingramcontent.com/pod-product-compliance
Lightning Source LLC
Chambersburg PA
CBHW011835020426
42335CB00022B/2826